Hexagon Quadrilateral

Hexagon Quadrilateral

CHRISTIAN ECONOMIC EMPOWERMENT

Kenneth Walley

CIBUNET
Publishing

Hexagon Quadrilateral

Published by
Cibunet Publishing
4-14 Saddle River Road Ste 204
Fair Lawn, Nj 07410
Email: admin@cibunet.com
Website: www.cibunet.com

TABLE OF CONTENTS

The Science of Understanding
Skillful In Wisdom
Productivity Pursuits

INTRODUCTION

T he scriptures are enshrined with several divine promises to believers who are diligent in their faith, and yet most of the giant corporations engaged in banking, retail, media manufacturing, oil exploration, mining etc. are owned by non-Christians. Majority of Christians only work as employees with no job security, which points to the fact that most Christians are obviously on the other side of the equation of financial prosperity. The major players in the world are somehow united in their resolve and tactics by which they hold on to the world's resources. Economic statistics indicate that one percent of the world control most of the financial resources of this world. A reversal of this trend would require a major shift in the mindset of Christians as it pertains to wealth.

First, wealth empowerment would only take place because divine judgment is in our favor. Second, the Churches, Christian owned organizations and believers must have a united front to uphold the biblical model that fosters wealth transfer in our favor. Third, as Christians, we must employ the scriptures in our professional endeavors to win the economic war against the kingdom of darkness.

I sense that these three factors that would orchestrate wealth transfer in favor believers are already unraveling. Recently, I received prophetic revelations about an impending failure of worldly structures by which the enemy exploits God's people. Jesus taught that to outwit an enemy we need to know their strengths and strategize accordingly. Some years ago, I was divinely convicted to employ information technology to establish an interactive system for economic empowerment which is known as 'Cibunet'. This system is loaded with hundreds of industry resources and company profiles which are regularly updated with current developments in each industry. This way, we pitch ourselves in the light of divine principles, credible facts about non-Christian corporate competitors and collaborate as Christians to emerge as leaders in the various areas of economic activity.

The Biblical Wealth Model

Through Moses, God delivered the Israelites from bondage in Egypt, and they headed toward the Promised Land of Canaan. At the threshold of the Promised Land, God required Moses to send the tribal leaders to spy out the land. "And the Lord spoke to Moses, saying, "Send men to spy out the land of Canaan, which I am giving to the children of Israel; from each tribe of their fathers you shall send a man, everyone a leader among them." So Moses sent them from the Wilderness of Paran according to the command of the Lord, all of them men who were heads of the children of Israel.... Then Moses sent them to spy out the land of Canaan, and said to them, "Go up this way into the South, and go up to the mountains, and see what the land is like: whether the people who dwell in it are strong or weak, few or many; whether the land they dwell in is good or bad; whether the cities they inhabit are like camps or strongholds; whether the land is rich or poor; and whether there are forests there or not. Be of good courage. And bring some of the fruit of the land." Now the time was the season of the first ripe grapes." Numbers 13:1-3, 17-20

Moses mandated the twelve tribal leaders of Israel to go and appraise the conditions of the Promised Land. They were to go through the south, which signifies the physical realm, and to the mountaintop, signifying the spiritual realm. The process for developing a good plan is as much a physical exercise as a spiritual one. Arriving at a good plan requires both scientific and spiritual analysis. It adapts divine principles and purposes in the light of a contemporary business environment. Moses required them to identify the characteristics of the Promised Land. The instruction to observe whether the people are 'strong or weak' indicates the human resource potentials of the Promised Land. 'Many or few' people reveal the marketing potentials. 'Good or bad land' reflects the corporate potentials. 'Tents or stronghold cities' are clues to the financial potentials. 'Fat or lean lands' depict productivity capabilities. 'Forest or grasslands' reveal the mission potentials. These characteristics of the Promised Land constitute the concepts by which this book is chaptered. My aim is that the principles set forth would provide the biblical foundation for developing a master plan for Christian economic empowerment.

Prior to Israel's conquest, the heathen inhabitants of the Promised Land were idol worshippers and so they subscribed to demonic practices. God explicitly instructed the Israelites to abolish such practices in the Promised Land. "When the Lord your God brings you into the land which you go to possess, and has cast out many nations before you, the Hittites and the Girgashites and the Amorites and the Canaanites and the Perizzites and the Hivites and the Jebusites, seven nations greater and mightier than you, and when the Lord your God delivers them over to you, you shall conquer them and utterly destroy them. You shall make no covenant with them nor show mercy to them... But thus you shall deal with them: you shall destroy their altars, and break down their sacred pillars, and cut down their wooden images, and burn their carved images with fire." Deuteronomy 7:1,2,5

The Apostle Paul in the New Testament puts it this way: "For though we walk in the flesh, we do not war according to the flesh. For the weapons of our warfare are not carnal but mighty in God for pulling down strongholds, casting down arguments and every high thing that exalts itself against the knowledge of God, bringing every thought into captivity to the obedience of Christ, and being ready to punish all disobedience when your obedience is fulfilled." 2 Corinthians 10:3-6

The following are the four aspects of a demonic stronghold:

- Worldly Principles
- Worldly Purposes
- Worldly Plans
- Worldly Pursuits

To destroy a demonic stronghold entail replacing each of the four aspects with:

- Divine Principles
- Divine Purposes
- Godly Plans
- Godly Pursuits

There is a scripture account in Genesis 26 of a famine during the lifetime of Isaac. A famine is the ancient version of economic hard times. As was the usual practice, Isaac decided to migrate to Egypt where the economic conditions were favorable. However, God forbade him to relocate and that he should remain in the land. With the condition of famine still persistent, the livestock of Isaac were growing lean and possibly dying. Though he was primarily a livestock farmer,

11

Isaac got creative and started cultivating the land to grow crops to feed the livestock.

"Then Isaac sowed in that land and reaped in the same year a hundredfold; and the Lord blessed him. The man began to prosper, and continued prospering until he became very prosperous; for he had possessions of flocks and possessions of herds and a great number of servants. So the Philistines envied him." (12-14)

Isaac became very prosperous in the land he was almost ready to abandon. The reason for the famine was because when his father Abraham died, Isaac did not contend for the wells which Abraham had dug. Failure to preserve values that are handed from previous generations could become the basis of a generational curse!

"Now the Philistines had stopped up all the wells which his father's servants had dug in the days of Abraham his father, and they had filled them with earth. And Abimelech said to Isaac, "Go away from us, for you are much mightier than we." Then Isaac departed from there and pitched his tent in the Valley of Gerar, and dwelt there." (15-17)

Though the Philistines became hostile to him and gave him reason to leave the land, Isaac moved away from their proximity and yet remained in the land as God had instructed him.

"And Isaac dug again the wells of water which they had dug in the days of Abraham his father, for the Philistines had stopped them up after the death of Abraham. He called them by the names which his father had called them." (18)

Isaac realized the reason for the famine and so he begun to revoke the generational curse. He revived the four wells of his father Abraham. These were the wells of Divine Principles, Divine Purposes, Godly Planning and Godly Pursuits.

Principles

"Also, Isaac's servants dug in the valley, and found a well of running water there. But the herdsmen of Gerar quarreled with Isaac's herdsmen, saying, "The water is ours." So he called the name of the well Esek, because they quarreled with him." (19-20)

The principles by which an enterprise is run is either worldly or divine. If you have paid attention to the trends of the business world over the last two hundred years, you will notice a pattern. Several principles of business practice that were glorified are gradually frowned upon and phased out. Examples are hoarding, profiteering, exploiting employees and most recently environmental depletion. These are all taught in the scriptures as divine principles by which the believer is expected to conduct his work and enterprise.

Whenever the world starts embracing a divine principle, it no longer becomes a competitive point for the believer. This is what happened when the Philistines contended with Isaac's herdsmen over the well 'Esek' that he had revived.

Purposes
"Then they dug another well, and they quarreled over that one also. So he called its name Sitnah." (21)

An enterprise is either established to primarily make money or in pursuit of divine purpose. When the fundamental enterprise goal is to make money, the leadership are constantly on the lookout for greener pastures. On the other hand, if the core goal of the enterprise is the pursuit of divine purpose, the leadership constantly finds ways to entrench the foundations of the enterprise as well as seek creative ways of growth. When Isaac realized that the Philistines started competing with him based on principles, he raised the bar and revived the well of purpose which was called 'Sitnah'. Here again, the Philistines rethought their enterprise goals and begun to compete by leveraging vertical and horizontal integrations.

Plans
"And he moved from there and dug another well, and they did not quarrel over it. So he called its name Rehoboth, because he said, "For now the Lord has

made room for us, and we shall be fruitful in the land."
(22)

Overcoming competition with cutting-edge strategies
is an important reality for any organization. Enterprise
plans are either worldly or godly. Worldly plans show
how you intend to achieve goals in the light of past and
present trends as well as future projections. Godly
plans engage such due diligence and incorporate divine
principles and purposes to formulate strategies. This is
where the believer breaks out ahead of the competition!
Isaac revived another well by name 'Rehoboth' - "For
now the Lord has made room for us, and we shall be
fruitful in the land."

Pursuits
"Then he went up from there to Beersheba. And the
Lord appeared to him the same night and said, "I am
the God of your father Abraham; do not fear, for I am
with you. I will bless you and multiply your descendants
for My servant Abraham's sake." So he built an altar
there and called on the name of the Lord, and he
pitched his tent there; and there Isaac's servants dug a
well. Then Abimelech came to him from Gerar with
Ahuzzath, one of his friends, and Phichol the
commander of his army. And Isaac said to them, "Why
have you come to me, since you hate me and have sent
me away from you?" But they said, "We have certainly
seen that the Lord is with you. So we said, 'Let there

now be an oath between us, between you and us; and let us make a covenant with you, that you will do us no harm, since we have not touched you, and since we have done nothing to you but good and have sent you away in peace. You are now the blessed of the Lord.'" So he made them a feast, and they ate and drank. Then they arose early in the morning and swore an oath with one another; and Isaac sent them away, and they departed from him in peace. It came to pass the same day that Isaac's servants came and told him about the well which they had dug, and said to him, "We have found water." So he called it Shebah. Therefore, the name of the city is Beersheba to this day." (23-33)

Pursuits are how we implement our plans. Here again, we can be either worldly in our approach or godly. Mergers, Acquisitions, Joint-ventures, Syndications, Consortiums are traditional ways of enterprise pursuit. Assuming this is done right and there are no hidden agendas or undisclosed pitfalls, they undergird the growth of an enterprise. Godly pursuits are mindful of the danger of unequal yoking and so covenant pursuits are prayerfully pursued. Though Isaac was now fruitful and the competition had backed away, he started out to revive the last of the four wells. Convinced that they were no match for Isaac's success, the Philistines came to seek a covenant relationship with him. Isaac knew that as owners of the land where God wanted him to be resident at the time, the land of the Philistines was the divine place for him and so he entered a covenant relationship with them. The fourth well 'Shebah' meaning covenant was revived at this point.

In this book we shall be looking at the six benchmarks for endeavoring in a venture against the premise of divine principles, purposes, planning and pursuits as well as the role of the Church in fostering overall prosperity for Believers in pursuit of their financial destiny.

Hexagon Quadrilateral

CHAPTER
1

Mission
Forests or Grasslands

"The righteous shall flourish like the palm tree:
he shall grow like a cedar in Lebanon"
Psalm 92:12

One of the benchmarks that was given to the tribal
leaders who were tasked with conducting a feasibility
study of the Promised Land was to check if there were
trees or it was a grassland. Forests are usually self-
sustaining ecosystems and trees were the means of

building estates and establishing industries. They are significant of enterprises that would thrive for the long haul. That is how our mission is divinely designed to be.

The body of Christ today comprises of businessmen, lawyers, politicians, judges, bankers, doctors, engineers, teachers, and other people who represent all professions. While some of these people are highly placed in government positions and corporations, some own large enterprises and others have massive investments in property and real estate. Clearly the church is a haven of great people with the potential for harvesting the wealth of the world to advance the gospel.

Spiritually, the church is like a forest filled with trees and many Christians can boast of giant strides in life because of living in righteousness. However, when it comes to our corporate economic status as believers in relation to the world, we are like trees scattered in the wilderness of financial frustration. The spirit of unity by which we prayerfully invoke God's presence in our worship is absent in our wealth pursuits. When the apostles sought God with 'one accord and in one place' on the day of Pentecost, there was an outpouring of the Holy Spirit that ushered a mighty move of God here on earth. Despite the awesome spiritual breakthrough that manifested through this outpouring of the Holy Spirit, poverty was still prevalent among the new believers. To overcome mediocrity, the apostles employed the same principles that ushered in the outpouring of the Holy Spirit. "And the multitude of them that believed were of one heart and of one soul: neither said any of them that ought of the things which he possessed was his own; but they had all things in common" Acts 4:32. With one heart and soul poverty was overcome by these believers. Agreement was the key. To overcome financial frustration, Christians in the local church must arise to the place of 'one heart and one soul'. We must eliminate prejudice in any form whether it is educational status, financial, professional, gender or color. Through the blood of Christ Jesus our past sins are forgiven and we all have the privilege of a new beginning with God. It is incumbent upon Christians in the local church to accord one another the trust and confidence of working together to achieve a common goal that is, victory over economic hardships.

Mission Ideology

"For there is hope of a tree, if it be cut down, that it will sprout again, and that the tender branch thereof will not cease. Though the root thereof wax old in the earth, and the stock thereof die in the ground; Yet through the scent of water it will bud, and bring forth boughs like a plant" Job 14:7-9

The prevalent mission ideology of the world is 'follow the money'. This means that you are constantly 'shifting grounds' regarding the mission of the enterprise. Here, you grab any opportunity to make money though this may not align with your core mission. When I worked as a Marbles and Granite contractor, I secured a contract to install marbles and granite for both interiors and exterior of a huge edifice. The client required us to start the interior installation immediately but then the ceilings had not been completed. The client couldn't find the services of a 'Plaster of Paris' ceiling contractor to execute the job so we could not proceed with granite floor installation. When I mentioned the challenge of the client to my business partner, he was furious. He contended that this was an opportunity to make more money. He insisted that I should take up the 'Plaster of Paris' ceiling contract and then sub-contract it. I secured the ceiling contract and sub-contracted it to a familiar client. The job was poorly executed and so it was disapproved. I engaged another ceiling contractor and again the job was disapproved. I became grieved in my spirit and so I sought the Lord, and He showed me that in the spirit realm, a snake had coiled itself to the ceiling so that the lines could never be straight. I probed further and the Lord said my mission was marbles and granite and that He had not assigned me to engage in 'Plaster of Paris' ceilings. Our marble and granite installations were approved but we took a loss for the ceiling contract as we had to relinquish that contract and forfeit the advance. 'Following the money' in the short or even medium term may seem a plausible strategy, but not in the long term. Such a philosophy is always the casualty of economic downturns which are an inevitable part of an economic cycle.

On the other hand, the mission ideology of the believer is to 'follow the water'. The water is the stream of divine convictions, revelations, and insights that a believer is privileged to receive through consistent fellowship with God. The believer is part of heaven's economy and shielded from the cycles of the world's economies. "God is our refuge and strength, a very present help in trouble. Therefore, will not we fear, though the earth be removed, and though the mountains be carried into the midst of the sea; Though the waters thereof roar and be troubled, though the mountains shake with the swelling thereof. There is a river, the streams whereof shall make glad the city of God, the holy place of the tabernacles of the Most High. God is in the midst of her; she shall not be moved: God shall help her, and that right early. The heathen raged, the kingdoms were moved: he uttered his voice, the earth melted. The Lord of hosts is with us; the God of Jacob is our refuge. Come, behold the works of the Lord, what desolations he hath made in the earth. He makes wars to cease unto the end of the earth; he breaks the bow and cuts the spear in sunder; he burns the chariot in the fire. Be still and know that I am God: I will be exalted among the heathen, I will be exalted in the earth. The Lord of hosts is with us; the God of Jacob is our refuge." Psalms 46. Our salvation in Christ assigns us an inheritance in His kingdom. This inheritance is the mission space where we exercise stewardship and dominion. The patriarchs from Adam until Moses were given their space without the need to fight for it so God taught them the concept of prospering in a space. Adam and Eve were created in the Garden of Eden that was sustained by four river heads – Pison, Gihon, Hiddekel and Euphrates. God taught Abraham to dig four wells for sustenance in times of drought. Isaac his son did not contend for these wells and so he suffered the consequences of drought until he revived these four wells dug originally by his father Abraham – Esek, Sitnah, Rehoboth and Beersheba. Streams that issue out of the city of God as we learn in the Psalm above unveil how the believer is designed to be sustained through the unpredictable cycles of our environments. Our mission synchronizes our work with God's work and makes us responsive to the generational challenges of our era.

Mission Principles

"You shall not sow your vineyard with different kinds of seed, lest the yield of the seed which you have sown, and the fruit of your vineyard be defiled." Deuteronomy 22:9

The seeds a farmer sows in a field, or the materials for constructing a building are the values of a mission. Such values are either worldly or godly. To mix both worldly and godly values produce mixed results. "Therefore, everyone who hears these words of mine and puts them into practice is like a wise man who built his house on the rock. The rain came down, the streams rose, and the winds blew and beat against that house; yet it did not fall, because it had its foundation on the rock. But everyone who hears these words of mine and does not put them into practice is like a foolish man who built his house on sand. The rain came down, the streams rose, and the winds blew and beat against that house, and it fell with a great crash." Matthew 7:24-27. A mission that would survive the unpredictable cycles of our economic environments is one that is founded upon godly values. Like a master craftsman diligently shopping for quality materials to make his work, every aspect of the mission must be carefully aligned with scriptural truths.

Mission Purpose

Determining your core mission could be anywhere from very simple to complicated. The process entails threading your entire life through the hole of a needle. If done correctly, you do not have to ever shift grounds, rather you would continue to grow roots downwards year after year. The mission of an enterprise is the harness of the burdens, passions, and revelations of the founders. Any mission function they assign the enterprise outside of themselves becomes an albatross. Mission is an interface of the burdens, passions, and revelations of the entrepreneur. This interface is how you determine your niche.

Burdens: The Prophet Habakkuk was burdened with the deplorable environment of the nation of Israel at one of its low points. "The burden which the prophet Habakkuk saw. O Lord, how long shall I cry, And You will not hear? Even cry out to You, "Violence!" And You will not save. Why do You show me iniquity, And cause me to see trouble? For plundering and violence are before me; There is strife, and contention arises. Therefore, the law is powerless, and justice never goes forth. For the wicked surround the righteous; Therefore, perverse judgment proceeds." Habakkuk 1:1-4. There is usually a challenging situation that shrouds our destiny assignment. It could be a circumstance that we would want changed at all costs. The inherent quest to tackle such a burden aligns our mission focus. "And they that shall be of you shall build the old waste places: you shall raise up the foundations of many generations; and you shall be called, The repairer of the breach, The restorer of paths to dwell in." Isaiah 58:12. The burden of a mission is usually ancestral. Every bloodline has divine mandates that are either fulfilled or neglected. God made a covenant with Abraham, ratified it in Isaac, confirmed it with Jacob and fulfilled in the tenures of Moses and Joshua. This same covenant is the basis of our blessings of redemption in Christ. It is interesting to note that Joseph the patriarch and son of Jacob did not end up in Egypt by accident. It was the beginning of the fulfilment of the covenant God made with his ancestor Abraham. God had said Abraham's descendants would be in Egypt for four hundred years. Moses killed an Egyptian who oppressed an Israelite as responsiveness to his ancestral burden for Israel. The mission of our inheritance space in Christ is how we get to fix the ancestral neglects, dysfunctions, breaches that could be basis of inherent poverty. As a believer whatever you choose to embark on as a mission must somehow tackle your ancestral assignment.

Passions: The Israelites of Habakkuk's day were unusually passionate about oppressing one another. "Indeed, because he transgresses by wine, He is a proud man, And he does not stay at home. Because he enlarges his desire as hell, and he is like death, and cannot be satisfied, He gathers to himself all nations And heaps up for himself all peoples. "Will not all these take up a proverb against him, And a taunting riddle against him, and say, 'Woe to him who increases What is not his—how long? And to him who loads himself with many pledges'? Will not your creditors rise up suddenly? Will they not awaken who oppress you? And you will become their booty. Because you have plundered many nations, All the remnant of the people shall plunder you, Because of men's blood And the violence of the land and the city, And of all who dwell in it. "Woe to him who covets evil gain for his house, that he may set his nest on high, That he may be

27

delivered from the power of disaster! You give shameful counsel to your house, Cutting off many peoples, And sin against your soul. For the stone will cry out from the wall, And the beam from the timbers will answer it. "Woe to him who builds a town with bloodshed, Who establishes a city by iniquity! Behold, is it not of the Lord of hosts that the peoples labor to feed the fire, And nations weary themselves in vain?" Habakkuk 2:5-13. The accepted norms, traditions and cultural practices of an era can fuel what people become passionate about. With the winds behind its sail, there is a general sense of support and consequent energy that sustains pursuit. Moses exhibited his leadership passion when he attempted to adjudicate an issue between two Israelites. King David was a passionate minstrel and wrote many psalms. King Solomon was very passionate about wisdom and researched how the world worked.

Revelations: To become a channel through whom God would change the state of society, Habakkuk sought God for a revelation. "I will stand upon my watch, and set me upon the tower, and will watch to see what he will say unto me, and what I shall answer when I am reproved. And the Lord answered me, and said, Write the vision, and make it plain upon tables, that he may run that reads it. For the vision is yet for an appointed time, but at the end it shall speak, and not lie: though it tarry, wait for it; because it will surely come, it will not tarry." Habakkuk 2:1-3. Revelations are the various convictions, dreams, visions, and prophecies we receive over time. They represent the input of heaven to guide our mission assignments. Revelation isolates potential vagueness and provides clarity about one's mission.

While burdens are those challenges that we feel obligated to resolve, passions are those activities for which we have unlimited energy, and for any mission, divine revelation is the ultimate seal of approval. Finding your mission niche is a vital task that helps define your enterprise and keep you focused. "Again, the kingdom of heaven is like a merchant seeking beautiful pearls, who, when he had found one pearl of great price, went and sold all that he had and bought it." Matthew 13:45-46. The melting point between your burden, passion and revelations carves out your specialization. It distinguishes your mission from others in the industry and becomes your basis of competition.

Lectad Enterprises had secured a large trade loan, and yet at the time their first interest payment was due, their entire capital was tied up with inventory at their warehouses. Business was slow, and the CEO was desperate. She mentioned her predicament to a member of my local Church, and he referred her to me. I requested a tour of the company outlets and warehouses to familiarize with their operations. Based on the concepts I have taught in this section, we proceeded to refocus the mission to reflect the burden, passion, and revelation of the company. The results were dramatic, and the company evaded being delinquent on the loan.

Assuming you are currently employed in an organization where you may be earning a comfortable salary but then your job has no element of your burden, passion, or revelation, you are doing yourself a great disfavor. You are neither entrenched in divine purpose nor are you insulated against a potential lay-off. Though you may have to take a step-down in salary, redeem yourself quickly from such potential redundancy and redeploy to any department that gives you the opportunity to serve in the arena of your burden, passion, or revelations.

My Burdens, Passions and Revelations: Growing up as a young boy in high school, I remember how passionate I was about economic news. If the headlines of the daily newspapers had a subject on the economy, I would read the article. I listened to the national budget, engaged neighbors who were professionals in discussions about the economy and always dreamed of becoming an industrialist someday. While in the final year of high school, I partnered with my elder brother Benny to start a food processing business. After high school I traveled internationally trading in various merchandise such as electronics, video tapes, jewelry etc. I enrolled in a business school where I studied advanced Economics, Business Management and Business Law. I got saved in my final year of high school but did not develop my relationship with God until I was in college. I started reading books authored by well renown bible teacher Derek Prince to develop my faith in the Lord. On one occasion while on campus and reading his book about obedience to the Holy Spirit, the Holy Spirit spoke to me for the first time. He instructed me to enter a lecture hall and I obeyed. He told me to lie down on the pew-like chairs and though I was uncomfortable with the instruction, I obeyed. As I laid down, I fell into a deep sleep and had a vision where I was at an auto workshop with my friend Peter.

In the vision, Peter proposed that we start a marketing enterprise together and since he was a marketing professional, he would handle that aspect of the business. I responded by suggesting becoming the administrator of the business. The following day, I decided to walk to Church for the midweek service and when I got to Peter's neighborhood, I decided to check on him. When I knocked the door of his apartment, he came out and blurted out "Ken, I have been looking for you". He grabbed his car keys and drove me to the exact auto workshop I had seen in my vision the previous day. He proposed that we start a marketing enterprise and that he would be responsible for marketing, and I also proposed to be responsible for the administration of the business. After this exchange I immediately realized that the vision of the previous day had manifested. That is how I got into business with Peter and the Lord opened doors for distributorship and other opportunities that were divinely promised.

I aspired to help teach Sunday School at Church, so I would diligently study the scriptures before office hours. One morning, as I was seated behind my desk reading my bible at the office of Ken and Peter Associates, I heard the Lord say: "Pastor Walley" and I was startled. I thought this was a mistake, so I immediately stood up and went to sit on the guest chair. As I continued to read the scriptures, suddenly the scriptures started jumping out to me in the form of a vision. Then I heard the Lord say: "Pastor Walley, don't you see how simple I have made my word to you?" I argued with the Lord that he had given me a business and so that was my destiny. He revealed to me that the business was to prove to me that He could do whatever He promises.

Not long after this encounter, the Lord instructed me on how He was going to train me for ministry and for three years I was trained. I started functioning as a Pastor and totally forgot my passion for business until one day while waiting upon the Lord, He told me that I was not a regular Pastor, and that He had called me to teach Christian Finance. I set time aside to wait upon Him and He taught me the divine principles of business and mandated me to hold seminars on the subject.

As a pastor and founding executive of the Christian Chamber of Commerce in Dallas, Texas, I and the president Tim Lynch and others travelled across the United States holding seminars in Churches and hotel venues. I travelled internationally for some of the business seminars and over the years I have been a consultant for various for-profit and non-profit enterprises. I have also successfully endeavored in business ventures such as Marble and Granite, Fuels and Lubricants and several others. Through my endeavors, I became strongly burdened with the failure of so many Christians who ventured into business with the underlining cause being the lack of professional support systems. I realized that those who succeeded in their pursuit of their destiny mission were either blessed to have a natural support system to lean on or could afford the services of professional consultants.

In the year 2000, I had a vision from God where He showed me the poverty in the nations of the world with a focus on the United States. Then He said to me, "The poverty in the world would not be overcome unless you engage the principle of economic segmentation". This vision as well as my exchanges with entrepreneurs at our seminars became the basis upon which I started Cibunet Corporation and begun developing the online platform based on the concept of economic segmentation. Divine principles of business are woven into every aspect of the system so that the believer engaging the system becomes compliant. The Cibunet platform is segmented into twenty-four core industries and subscribers choose where they belong. Subscribers have access to industry-specific resources, business tools for planning, funding and management of projects and enterprises. Today, Cibunet is helping Christian entrepreneurs and start-ups with Business Development Support while Churches are helped with Economic Empowerment Team Development. The journey of developing the concepts for the Cibunet platform has been over three decades in making!

Mission Plans

Several years ago, I served in the leadership of an evangelistic outreach ministry that held mass crusades to various communities. Before I joined this group, they held an average of two crusades annually. I introduced concepts that quickly mushroomed the number of crusades to a monthly basis. The leader of another evangelistic outreach ministry with greater resources begun to wonder how we were able to hold so many crusades knowing the high cost of such meetings. Some of his lieutenants mentioned that I was responsible, so he arranged to meet me for consultation. That is how I built a reputation for helping ministries overcome administrative challenges as well as expand their operations.

Prior to Moses, the patriarchs did not have need to conquer the space they occupied. However, after exiting Egypt, and now at the threshold of the

34

Promised Land, Israel had to apply the concepts by which a space is conquered. "Again, the kingdom of heaven is like treasure hidden in a field, which a man found and hid; and for joy over it he goes and sells all that he has and buys that field." Matthew 13:44. The promise of an inheritance in Christ and the concepts by which one takes over this space is the treasure hidden in a field. Various strategic concepts are necessary to conquer a space. God required the leaders of the twelve tribes to conduct a feasibility study of the Promised Land based on six benchmarks. These benchmarks of Mission, Human Resource, Corporate Resource, Productivity, Market and Finance would become the basis for their plan. A plan for conquest of a space entails goals and strategies developed, using the facts collected through the feasibility study. Ultimately, the plan for conquest should entail six core goals and strategies to accomplish each of them. Jesus Christ taught the essence of strategy: "Suppose one of you wants to build a tower. Won't you first sit down and estimate the cost to see if you have enough money to complete it? For if you lay the foundation and are not able to finish it, everyone who sees it will ridicule you, saying, 'This person began to build and wasn't able to finish.' "Or suppose a king is about to go to war against another king. Won't he first sit down and consider whether he is able with ten thousand men to oppose the one coming against him with twenty thousand? If he is not able, he will send a delegation while the other is still a long way off and will ask for terms of peace."

Luke 14:28-32. Jesus teaches that the building of a tower and waging war requires planning and strategy. A typical mission would require the essence of conquering a space and building it up to serve its purpose. Planning is a diligence that usually requires less money than the actual cost of execution and yet is so vital to the success of the mission. Many people think of planning only in a narrow way such as saving up money to pay for the costs of the project or enterprise or war. Though saving up resources for executing the mission is important, it is often the last puzzle in the process of planning. In the same way that an architect requires surveys for his drawings and miliary generals require military intelligence reports to develop war strategy, a feasibility study is indispensable for a mission. A good plan first requires a feasibility study to evaluate the mission field based on the six benchmarks. Here, we endeavor to observe how others in the same mission field tackle their challenges and opportunities. Core goals are set. Each of these goals would require a strategy. Strategy is the method by which available resources are harnessed to tackle known challenges on the mission field. Here, we take cognizance of all elements required to conquer as well as build up the space. Effective strategy leverages creative methods to deploy the least amount of resources to accomplish the set goals.

Mission Plan Dynamics - "As long as the earth endures, seedtime and harvest, cold and heat, summer and winter, day and night will never cease." Genesis 8:22

Before any mention of rainfall, the scriptures tell of a mist that watered the earth as well as rivers that flowed from the Garden of Eden. Noah's prediction of rainfall would have certainly sounded a strange phenomenon to those of his generation. The rainfall became a flood that wiped out that generation except for those with Noah in the ark. After the flood, Noah offered sacrifices to God that triggered the divine enactment of four precedents that established a predictable ecosystem that is a dynamic for planning any endeavor.

Day and Night – Standards: The day signifies righteousness while night signifies unrighteousness. A mission plan must be enshrined with values that distinguish righteousness from unrighteousness. The mission must clearly define standards that would be upheld by everyone in the organization.

Cold and Heat – Renaissance: Cold is a metaphor for apostasy while heat signifies revival. A good mission plan must aim at a renaissance of certain abandoned purposes. These redemptive purposes must be well articulated in the mission plan.

Seedtime and Harvest – Creativity: Seed is the cultivation of something new while harvest is the reaping of what is sown. The mission plan must inculcate creative methods for both productivity and marketing, otherwise the mission may not survive the test of competition.

Summer and Winter – Tranquility: Summer is the best weather season where we can achieve outdoor objectives while winter is the austere season that forces us indoors. A good mission plan lays out unique tactics for harnessing opportunities of the summertime to overcome the challenges of the wintertime.

Mission Pursuits

Pursuit is how you accomplish objectives by leveraging covenants, alliances, opportunities with unique tactics. God's covenant with Abraham guided the decisions and alliances of Abraham during his lifetime. After the death of Abraham, there was a famine in the land and Isaac intended to relocate to Egypt. The Lord restrained Isaac, reminding him of the divine covenant with Abraham. Isaac became very successful in the land of the Philistines where God directed him to reside. Based upon this same divine covenant, Isaac agreed to a proposal of alliance by Abimelech the Philistine king. According to God's covenant with Abraham, his descendants would be strangers in a foreign nation for four hundred years and return to possess the land of the Canaanites. Joseph the great grandson of Abraham had dreams of global leadership that triggered the hatred of his brothers. They sold him to slavery, and he ended up in Egypt. Though this was an austere challenge for Joseph, it was a fulfilment of a part of God's covenant with Abraham. Joseph eventually rose to become prime minister of Egypt and his father Jacob with the entire family emigrated to join him there.

When we occupy the space of our inheritance in Christ, various challenges and opportunities would manifest in their due season. These are divine orchestrations that give indication of the 'kairos' right time which we must learn to take advantage of. Whenever a challenge occurs, it is also signal to opportunities in the horizon. We ought not to shy away from these challenges but rather tackle them by faith, trusting that the corresponding opportunities to administer such have been divinely furnished. Each time a challenge or opportunity comes knocking at our door, the strategies formulated in our plans become the basis for our tactics. Tactics are the unique ways by which we implement our objectives. They are the mission policies and procedures we establish for our various departments. These policies and procedures must certainly incorporate our divine values, convictions and perceptions.

Blind Enterprises: Where people of different persuasions partner as founders of an enterprise, a blind entity is formed and there can be no original mission. First, mainstream ideals are not always righteous and may be outright oppressive. The issue with boards constituted with members of different values systems is that some members in seeking relevance usually propose concepts emulated from other enterprises which tend to often kill original ideas. Second, the accepted norm is that a mission worth pursuing must be justified by trends. You will agree with me however, that many of the start-ups that have experienced phenomenal breakthroughs were mainly because of industry disruptions. Third, a strategy that simply seeks to make as much money as possible invokes the basest thinking of any human. In the high quest to make money today for instance, food that animals won't even eat are nicely packaged by corporations and sold to fellow humans, products with terrible side-effects are offered to the unsuspecting public and so on. Fourth, it is worth noting that a lot of the proposed mergers and acquisitions by major enterprises are geared toward oligopoly where there are a few sellers in an industry with the ulterior motive of trampling upon consumers.

Hexagon Quadrilateral

Hexagon Quadrilateral

CHAPTER
2

Human Resource
Strong Or Weak People

W ith a population of over a billion people, China is overcoming the stigma of poverty that was characteristic of this overpopulated nation some years ago. Instead of dwelling on their problems of overpopulation as a reason to be poor, they simply harnessed their numbers as a valuable factor of production. Today China is one of the leading industrialized nations in the world. Moses instructed the twelve tribal leaders who were undertaking a feasibility study of the Promised Land, to take note of 'the people that dwell therein, whether they be strong or weak'. Wherever weak people gather themselves is an indication of chronic failures. Strong people are usually described as giants. Giants are those who have distinguished themselves as authorities in specific vocations or as champions in certain areas of pursuit. This is generally indicative of great human resource potentials.

I mentioned earlier that the Lord taught me the divine principles of business, but then I also did due diligence and furthered my education to obtain masters in Business Administration as well as Managerial Economics and Business Analysis. A substantive mission would require professional competence to administer. If unskilled people can accomplish your mission, there is a tendency that you will have a lot of unnecessary competition to deal with.

Any enterprise that stands the test of time should be comprised of a leadership team of giants. Each member of your team should be skillful and creative. Skill is the essence of having some form of training that is required for each role. Through their resume, it is easy to determine if a person has skills. However, creativity is the essence of being anointed for their role in the enterprise. This is harder to determine and so in the same way that Jesus prayed all-night to choose the twelve apostles, we must resort to prayerfully select creative people. The wrong people on your leadership team often becomes a pain in the long run.

Human Resource Principles

People generally complain and sometimes become counter-productive when they are not treated as fairly as they expect at the workplace. Godly principles are designed to create an atmosphere that enhances the productivity of our human resources. To attract the best caliber of workers and maintain them in our workforce, it is vital that we adopt the best working conditions possible.

Salaries & Wages: "You shall not defraud your neighbor, neither rob him: the wages of him that is hired shall not abide with you until the morning." Leviticus 19:13

The disparity between the wages of top executives and lower-level employees in many giant enterprises is ludicrous. Some top executives earn upwards of $10 million dollars while lower-level employees earn a meager $30,000 annually. In determining the wages of a worker, we are required to be as fair as possible. Some employers take advantage of cheap labor when they can sufficiently remunerate employees. Also, certain employers are fond of unduly delaying the benefits of employees to invest the money for quick returns. This is a violation of the principles of remuneration, as it inflicts great suffering on the workers. Knowing fully well how much it costs a believer to be of service to you, it is important to appropriately remunerate them.

Fringe Benefits: "You shalt not muzzle the ox when he treads out the corn." Deuteronomy 25:4

We all get the privilege at some point to host workers employed by a contractor whom we may have engaged for home improvement, maintenance, or home care services. Though you may not have directly hired such workers, you must show hospitality in any way possible. The conditions of service in any organization should enable workers to draw some form of comfort from the job. Preventing the ox from eating while treading the corn is symbolic of taking undue advantage of labor. For instance, a worker who is sent out to accomplish a task should be given sufficient transport and travel allowance.

"When you come into thy neighbor's vineyard, then you may eat grapes to your fill at your own pleasure; but you shall not put any in your vessel." Deuteronomy 23:24

A free or subsidized meal at lunchtime during working hours is not too much for a prosperous business. The employer must improve work conditions as much as possible. In turn, employees must also not take undue advantage of the enterprise by stealing at the workplace.

Health Insurance: "If you see the donkey of him that hates thee lying under his burden, and would forbear to help him, you shall surely help him." Exodus 23:5

Many employees suffer health problems as a direct or indirect result from work. Health insurance for employees is a scriptural requirement. Many insurance companies offer programs and packages for corporate bodies to take responsibility for the health insurance of their workers. It only takes signing up and paying affordable monthly premiums to guarantee the health insurance of your human resource.

Hiring & Firing: "You shall not deliver unto his master the servant which is escaped from his master to you; He shall dwell with you, even among you, in that place which he shall choose in one of your gates, where it suits him best: you shall not oppress him." Deuteronomy 23:15-16

A Christian employer has the freedom to hire other Christians who have retired from other Christian owned organizations. Such employees must be granted the opportunity to work in the arena of their divine potentials. Maltreatment of employees is wrong.

Bond Service: "And if your brother that dwells by you become poor and be sold to you; you shall not compel him to serve as a bond servant; But as a hired servant and as a sojourner, he shall be with you, and shall serve you to the year of jubilee." Leviticus 25:39-40

The principle of bond service forbids Christians to demand that their employees sign up for bond service. A common example is when an employer sponsors an employee for specialized training. The employer usually asks the employee to sign a bond to serve for a specified number of years after the training. With non-Christian employees, such an arrangement is allowed but not so with fellow Christian employees.

A Healing Tree, Twelve Wells and Seventy Palms

"Now when they came to Marah, they could not drink the waters of Marah, for they were bitter. Therefore, the name of it was called Marah. And the people complained against Moses, saying, "What shall we drink?" So he cried out to the Lord, and the Lord showed him a tree. When he cast it into the waters, the waters were made sweet. There He made a statute and an ordinance for them, and there He tested them, and said, "If you diligently heed the voice of the Lord your God and do what is right in His sight, give ear to His commandments and keep all His statutes, I will put none of the diseases on you which I have brought on the Egyptians. For I am the Lord who heals you." Then they came to Elim, where there were twelve wells of water and seventy palm trees; so they camped there by the waters." Exodus 15:23-27

An important landmark on their journey from Egypt to the Promised Land was the crossing of the Red Sea. The Israelites travelled for three days and found no water. When they found water at Marah, it was bitter and could not be drank. Moses sought God and was directed to a tree which when he put in the water it became sweet. This is significant of the innermost core of any leadership. Jesus Christ had Peter, James, and John as those who constituted that core. As it were, they were His soul. He went with them to the mountain where He was transfigured in the meeting with Moses and Elijah. He charged them to keep the encounter a secret until later. Peter was the one to ascertain by revelation knowledge that Jesus was the Christ. When he is opposed to the cross, Jesus rebukes this ignorance and teaches the essence of every follower carrying their cross. Peter goes on to become the earthly leader of the New Testament Church. James and John are brothers who were very zealous for Christ. Their mother requests that Jesus position them in a place of prominence in the kingdom. Jesus rebukes the request and establishes humility and servanthood as the keys. Notice that these three had an unusual zeal for Christ which was somewhat carnally expressed, but then Jesus corrected them. Those who constitute the innermost core of your leadership usually have a single-hearted commitment to you. Their first instinct is often to defend you as much as is within their ability. They are divinely chosen to sustain your soul in difficult times and channel supernatural healing to your being. You can bounce off your ideas to them and gain a litmus test of how others would react to these new ideas.

At Elim there were twelve wells which are significant of government. Wells are generational reservoirs that sustain with water during times of drought. Jacob the father of the nation Israel had twelve sons by whom the tribes of Israel as well as their prophetic destines were established. Jesus had twelve disciples that were designated as Apostles. They were the leadership group that he set as official witnesses of His life, death, and resurrection. It is their testimony that are recorded in the synoptic gospels. Every enterprise has a board of directors as its governing body. Those who are chosen to constitute this body for a Christian enterprise must understand their core function as wells. They must pay keen attention to the revelations, passions, and burdens of the visionary. Their role is fundamentally apostolic, that is to consider every idea, opportunity, or challenge in the light of divine principles and purposes.

Also, at Elim there were seventy palm trees which are significant of fruitfulness by the anointing. When Moses felt overly burdened by his leadership responsibility, God anointed seventy leaders to share the burden. In addition to the twelve apostles, Jesus had another layer of leadership comprised of seventy disciples who were also empowered to fulfil the great commission. This third layer of leadership feeding off the twelve wells to bear fruit, is the concept of organically growing the mission outwards from the visionary. This way, the entire organization is like an organism that evolves from a cell nucleus, through the plasma and multiplies itself as growth. The entire human resource of your organization must be organically structured so everyone can bear the desired kind of fruit.

Human Resource Plan

When people are treated well and facilitated with the right working environment, they become resourceful and innovative, which ultimately drives the enterprise to its place of leadership in the industry. Chick-fil-A one of the leading fast-food restaurant chains in the US audaciously touts on its website and signposts: 'Why we're closed on Sundays'. According to their website, the founder, Truett Cathy, made the decision to close on Sundays in 1946 when he opened his first restaurant in Hapeville, Georgia. Having worked seven days a week in restaurants that open 24 hours, Truett saw the importance of closing on Sundays so that he and his employees could set aside one day to rest and worship if they choose — a practice they uphold today.

"Six days shall work be done: but the seventh day is the sabbath of rest, an holy convocation; ye shall do no work therein: it is the sabbath of the Lord in all your dwellings." Leviticus 23:3

Some of Cathy's most significant business decisions were made with employees in mind. For example, his decision to close on Sundays, a practice started to give restaurant employees (and himself) a day to rest. Cathy started the practice when he had only one restaurant, and as he opened new Chick-fil-A restaurants, the malls where his restaurants were located pressured Cathy to open on Sundays, but he refused. Chick-fil-A restaurant owners and team members knew they could count on one day each weekend that they could devote to resting, friends, family and personal pursuits. Cathy wanted them to find success. Not having the opportunity to attend college himself, Cathy established a college scholarship program in 1973 for restaurant team members. Cathy wanted to encourage restaurant employees to further their education. Over time, the scholarship program evolved to place greater emphasis on an employee's community service and leadership abilities. His goal was to propagate the qualities that would help them not only be successful in school, but also in life. After all, Chick-fil-A restaurants, Cathy believed, should be places where people develop into future leaders. In fact, his first gauge of his restaurant owners' success was not profits or sales, but the number of future Chick-fil-A restaurant owners that started their careers in that restaurant.

In his own first restaurant, the Dwarf House, Cathy earned a reputation for having a heart for his employees. Eddie White, a teenager working in the Dwarf House in the 1950s, hoped to attend college, but he needed financial help. The waitresses put an empty mayonnaise jar labeled "Eddie's College Fund" on the counter for customers, who felt like family, to fill up. In the fall of 1955, when it was time to start college, the jar had not collected enough, so Truett wrote a check for the difference and that was his first scholarship. White completed college and went on to a career as a classroom educator, and ultimately an assistant superintendent of a school system near Atlanta.

Human Resource Pursuits

"If your brother, a Hebrew man, or a Hebrew woman, is sold to you and serves you six years, then in the seventh year you shall let him go free from you. And when you send him away free from you, you shall not let him go away empty-handed; you shall supply him liberally from your flock, from your threshing floor, and from your winepress. From what the Lord your

God has blessed you with, you shall give to him. You shall remember that you were a slave in the land of Egypt, and the Lord your God redeemed you; therefore I command you this thing today. And if it happens that he says to you, 'I will not go away from you,' because he loves you and your house, since he prospers with you, then you shall take an awl and thrust it through his ear to the door, and he shall be your servant forever. Also to your female servant you shall do likewise. It shall not seem hard to you when you send him away free from you; for he has been worth a double hired servant in serving you six years. Then the Lord your God will bless you in all that you do." Deuteronomy 15:12-18

The seventh year sabbath commonly known as the Sabbatical was a period usually a year when God's people were required to refrain from working. It was intended as a release from all forms of labor bondage. Those Israelites who had sold themselves to work as slaves were released from bond service. They were provisioned by their masters with resources to help them revive their destiny assignments. This way, the release facilitated an organic way for God's people to find their way back to fulfil divine purpose. Those Israelites who were content with their service and unwilling to be released from their work were to enter a covenant relationship. Such people were either very pleased to continue working with the enterprise because of the good conditions of service or were not yet ready to pursue their own mission. Some of the practical ways of implementing the release is to establish Career Development Programs, Ownership and Wealth Building Opportunities for the human resources of the enterprise.

Though some may imagine that implementing the release could breed potential competitors, the pursuit of divine purpose makes everyone unique in their own mission. Hence every potential competitor may only end up serving a particular niche in the industry. Notice how in the past two hundred years so many subindustries have evolved from the basic industrial segments. From basic timepieces manufactured by the Swiss, today we have digital timepieces which are a cross-industrial function of engineering and information technology.

Turnover Rate: It is easy to determine the future of a firm with a simple question to their employees such as: "Do you love coming to work in this organization?" An employer who fails to treat employees as stakeholders of the enterprise has already failed the long-term strategy test. A high turnover rate of employee retention signals a bleak future for an enterprise. It is an indication of poor or unsatisfactory conditions of service that leaves employees discontented and unwilling to remain in such an environment. In the same way the entrepreneur pursues an enterprise to deploy potential, seeking profit and legacy, employees are looking for a place where their potentials are harnessed, appreciated as well as the sense of job security. If the human resource strategy of an enterprise addresses these core needs, it lowers the turnover rate of employee retention.

Hexagon Quadrilateral

Hexagon Quadrilateral

CHAPTER
3

CORPORATE RESOURCE
Good Or Bad Lands

U sing the gospel as bait, the British sent missionaries to many nations and eventually colonized them. This way, they guaranteed supply of cheap raw materials to feed their industrial revolution. Ultimately, Britain emerged as an economically powerful world leader for many years. Corporate resource is about who we are collectively, the values we cherish and the material resources that are naturally occurring in our environment. In their study of the

Promised Land, Moses required the tribal leaders to check the quality of the land 'whether it be good or bad'. Agriculture is the source of man's food. It thrives where the soil is good. Fertile land is an indication of potential prosperity since raw materials will be available for productivity. After the conquest of Canaan, the land was divided among the various tribes and families of Israel. Every allotment became the natural inheritance of subsequent generations of the various tribes and families. The natural resources in every allotment determined the occupation of the heirs. For instance, land rich in gold ore encouraged gold mining and gold smithery, while grasslands encouraged cattle farming and so on.

Corporate Values

Interstate Batteries is an outstanding Christian company that has boldly published on their website the values by which they operate. When John Searcy founded Interstate Batteries in 1952, his vision was for the company to help its team members, distributors and partners provide for their families and give back to their communities. Selling batteries was just a vehicle to accomplish a much broader goal. He wanted to make his company about something more than profits, to work in a way that would please God. John treated people as he would want to be treated and modeled this well to his whole team, including the Chairman Norm Miller. When Norm began to run the company in 1978, he held true to these ideals and within a few years Norm included "to glorify God" in the mission statement.

In 2013, they further defined their purpose and articulated a set of core values with input from all their key stakeholders:

Love - Treats others like you want to be treated.
Servants Heart - Lead with what people need.
Excellence - Do great things with the gifts you've been given.
Courage - Learn, improve, and boldly drive change that matters.
Fun - Work hard, laugh often.
Team - Together, we're better.
Integrity - Be who you are and live up to your commitments.

Interstate Batteries is a mission-driven company fueled by our Purpose (to glorify God) and guided by our Values (Love, Servant's Heart, Excellence, Courage, Team, Fun and Integrity). Interstate team members can expect a flexible work environment respectful of life-work balance that also offers opportunity to play a role in the transformation of a 68-year-old iconic brand. Our frequent (at least quarterly) team member engagement surveys tell us that Interstate team members value working for a company with a purpose greater than just making money or selling batteries.

Team members enjoy our workplace flexibility (the ability to work from home or leave early to attend children's events) and appreciate being able to bring their whole selves to a workplace that seeks to nourish not only their professional, but also their physical, emotional, and spiritual health. The ability to work on progressive, innovative, and often industry-changing projects also rates very highly on our surveys. We fulfill our purpose by doing business based on Biblical principles – such as honesty, humility, service, and care – in a way that is welcoming and loving to all. As a company contributor, you are free to interact with the purpose in whatever way is most meaningful to you. Our values, however, are unchanging, and we ask that our team members try their best to live them as they serve our key stakeholders: team members, customers, distributors and franchisees, suppliers and vendors, communities, and shareholders. By creating a welcoming and caring environment, we hope to create a positive experience for our team members and everyone else whom Interstate touches, no matter their background or belief system.

Tyson Foods is another notable enterprise that touts its Christian values on their website: "From the beginning, our company has been built on faith, family, and hard work. That tradition, our Core Values, and 'doing what's right' are deeply embedded in our culture." John Tyson, Chairman

Who We Are:
We strive to be honorable and operate with integrity.
We strive to be faith-friendly and inclusive.
We strive to serve as stewards of the resources entrusted to us.
We strive to provide a safe work environment
What We Do:
We feed our families, the nation, and the world with trusted food products.
We serve as stewards of the animals, land, and environment entrusted to us.
We strive to provide a safe work environment for our team members.

How We Do It:
We strive to earn consistent and satisfactory profits for our shareholders and to invest in our people, products, and processes.
We strive to operate with integrity and trust in all we do.
We strive to honor God and be respectful of each other, our customers, and other stakeholders.

Procurement Principles - It is a very common practice for shrewd businessmen to take advantage of desperate sellers by purchasing from them at rip off prices. "And if you sell anything to your neighbor, or buy anything of your neighbor's hand, ye shall not oppress one another" Leviticus 25:14. Through the shrewd practices of such businessmen, many sellers end up at a loss while the buyers re-sell at exorbitant prices. Such practices violate the principles of righteous purchasing. As much as your aim in business is to make profit, you should not drive producers and your suppliers out of business in the process. Middlemen in the business chain such as wholesalers, commodity traders and the like often fall short of this principle. Those who deliberately default on credit, though they can pay up, are also guilty of violating this principle.

Corporate Sustainability

In many communities across the world, raw materials are mined in a haphazard manner and the land left totally untenable. Travelling via local roadways through the interior of the US reveals an appalling image of communities that were literally raped by enterprises and abandoned. There are certain cities like New Delhi in India, where the pollution from factories and vehicles causes a blanket of thick smog over the atmosphere and some people wear masks to protect their lungs. Through irresponsible practices of many industrialists, the environment has decayed to the extent that the science community is calling for immediate action to reverse the trend.

"And God said, Let us make man in our image, after our likeness: and let them have dominion over the fish of the sea, and over the fowl of the air, and over the cattle, and over all the earth, and over every creeping thing that creeps upon the earth. So God created man in his own image, in the image of God created he him; male and female created he them. And God blessed them, and God said unto them, Be fruitful, and multiply, and replenish the earth, and subdue it: and have dominion over the fish of the sea, and over the fowl of the air, and over every living thing that moves upon the earth." Genesis 1:26-28

At creation, man was blessed with dominion over creation, to be fruitful and multiply. These we have done well but then one of the core mandates given man was to 'replenish the earth'. Our attitude has been as one trying to build a tall building without a foundation. We have altogether behaved as irresponsible custodians of the earth and yet some politicians blatantly refuse to acknowledge our folly.

Currently, some nations are rising to the challenge and working to reduce greenhouse emissions across the globe. Companies must publish a sustainability report that guarantees that their practices would not deplete the environment of their communities. Organizations touting green products are springing up everywhere because there is a new global consciousness of the need. There is still so much work to be done. Many corporations notably financial institutions and technology companies are still using the 'fine print' to rape customers. While it seems as the way to go for these companies, it serves as a strategic opening for Christian enterprises to take the lead.

Cultural Evolution

When you travel by train across North America, you will find dilapidated buildings that were previously thriving industries, wholesale, retail companies, hotels, and restaurants. Most of these companies were located along the tracks of the railroad because it was the predominant means of transportation and commercial life revolved around it. Today however, the story is different with the emergence of other forms of transportation such as the automobile highways and air travel. Commercial life no longer thrives exclusively around the railroad and those businesses which were unable to foresee these inevitable transitions ultimately failed.

Remember the term 'kodak-moments'. Not too long ago, Kodak, the company and film product was a household name synonymous with photography. Today, Kodak has sadly become history that is attributed to two factors that tend to make an enterprise irrelevant. First is ignorance of industry-specific trends and second is ignorance of cross-industrial trends. No industry exists in isolation. Kodak got complacent with their industry dominance and failed to pay attention with industry-specific as well as cross-industrial trends. They were eventually blind-sided and overrun by the information technology industry that was busy developing integrated digital applications surrounding social life that wowed consumers. It is detrimental to be overly focused on outwitting the obvious competition and ignore potentially disruptive cross-industrial hybrid innovations.

The Covid-19 global pandemic was a health crisis and yet it has had a far-reaching impact on every other industry either directly or indirectly. The global supply logistics crisis, unprecedented inflation among others are examples of cross-industrial challenges triggered by a health industry problem. Recently I was dropping off my eighteen-year-old daughter Adelph at school when on the way she mentioned the post-pandemic human resource trend of 'quiet quitting'. 'Quiet quitting' is to remain on a job only fulfilling the basic duties and not working hard above and beyond expectations to climb the corporate ladder. The pandemic has fostered a cultural shift that has given many people the opportunity to reflect on their careers and aspirations of life. For instance, it is no longer weird to work from home. Furthermore, the pandemic has catapulted the gig-economy into full swing, which facilitates more people to work as independent contractors in most industries. Geopolitical challenges such as the Russia-Ukraine war may have seemed a remote issue between two former Soviet Union states but then has significantly impacted the global food supply as well as triggered an energy crisis especially in Europe. Ukraine is one of the largest producers of wheat in the world while Russia supplies a big chunk of Europe's energy, so the logistic blockades and sanctions are adversely impacting many industries and the overall global economy.

Cultural intelligence is necessary for remaining relevant. This means that the both the product as well as the business model must continue to evolve dynamically. The mission, human resource, cultural resource, productivity, market, and finance strategies that comprise the business model must constantly progress with culture. For us Believers, there's a nuance between relevance and compromise that must be clearly distinguished. Relevance is how we synchronize our works with the process of time while compromise is to give up on our core values and divine convictions.

The movies 'The Ten Commandments' 'Jesus of Nazareth and 'The Passion of the Christ' are among the list of great movies that received and continue to be patronized by both believers and unbelievers alike. Historical events enshrined in the scriptures were dramatized and published through masterpiece movie-making systems. Some of these movies broke records when they were released and hauled in astronomical profits for their producers. Cultural relevance either positions you ahead of culture or in synch with it. "One generation passes away, and another generation comes; But the earth abides forever. The sun also rises, and the sun goes down, and hastens to the place where it arose. The wind goes toward the south and turns around to the north; The wind whirls about continually and comes again on its circuit. All the rivers run into the sea, Yet the sea is not full; To the place from which the rivers come, there they return again. All things are full of labor; Man cannot express it. The eye is not satisfied with seeing, Nor the ear filled with hearing. That which has been is what will be, That which is done is what will be done, And there is nothing new under the sun." Ecclesiastes 1:4-9 Culture is always spinning on an axis of past-present-future so there are some people who have been able to predict trends successfully to some extent. While unbelievers quickly jump on the wagon of whatever is trendy, our Christian values are the primary building blocks with which we accomplish a rock-solid mission. "Therefore, whoever hears these sayings of Mine, and does them, I will liken him to a wise man who built his house on the rock: and the rain descended, the floods came, and the winds blew and beat on that house; and it did not fall, for it was founded on the rock. "But everyone who hears these sayings of Mine, and does not do them, will be like a foolish man who built his house on the sand: and the rain descended, the floods came, and the winds blew and beat on that house; and it fell. And great was its fall." Matthew 7:24-27. Regardless of the trends, our relevance is defined by the values and convictions that align our mission with the times. We must cultivate the audacity to set the standards for future cultural shifts and redefine abhorrent trends. As believers, we don't only seek to be relevant but also strive to be resilient – bearing fruits upwards while growing roots downward at the same time.

At every point in time, we are either moving forward culturally or backwards. Culture being the values we collectively uphold, may tend to foster our overall progress or retrogression in society. In England today, most of the thriving Churches that history tells of, have now been converted into residential homes or offices. The reason is that the Church continued to preach an irrelevant message and archaic Christian culture did not transition with the changes in society. Today, there are thriving pubs in almost every area of England while very few English people attend Church.

God has a sovereign plan for the world and Satan's plan is to frustrate it at all costs. The history of trends of dark ages followed by renaissances, as well as spiritual apostasies followed by spiritual revivals, are evidence of this fact. In the introduction, I wrote about the famine in the days of Isaac and how he overcame by reviving the wells of his father Abraham. Abraham had experienced a famine during his life and the divine solution was to dig wells. However, when Abraham died, the Philistines seized these wells and filled them with earth to stop their flow of water. It sounds absurd that they should do this, however the attitude of Isaac was even worse. He did not contend for these wells. As it were, he equally did not value their significance. It was when God restrained him from relocating to Egypt that he started taking stock of what he could have been doing wrongly. When he realized it was his abandonment of his father's wells, that begun the revival that saved his enterprise. Like the Philistines of old, the kingdom of darkness constantly devises schemes to frustrate and terminate any principles, purposes and plans by which God intends to sustain human life. Our divine mandate as believers is to contend for the faith through our works in harmony with God's works. Though we could be employed at an organization that may not uphold righteous values, it is incumbent upon us as believers to demonstrate the righteous values of our faith in every way possible while at work.

Corporate Resource Pursuits

During research I conducted into the agro-commodity market in the United Kingdom, I found out how difficult it was for new entrants to penetrate the business of commodities. The major commodity brokers established contractual relationships with large-scale manufacturers and acted as exclusive supplies. This way such brokers had little or no competition in the procurement of crops from farmers. They paid very low prices for the crops and ripped off the poor farmers. A new manufacturer of coffee products, who realized how difficult it was to gain an entrance into the business, adopted the goodwill strategy of buying coffee beans directly from poor farmers in Africa and Asia. He then proceeded to advertise these goodwill gestures on every product to win the sentiments and consequent patronage of the consuming public. In every business endeavor, it is important to always remember that profit begins at the source. "Every prudent man acts out of knowledge" Proverbs 13:16. Prudence in purchasing means that one should firstly research, and then employ the kind of strategy that would ensure profit in procurement.

Hexagon Quadrilateral

Hexagon Quadrilateral

CHAPTER
4

Productivity
Fat Or Lean Lands

In almost every home across the world today, you will find at least a product with the brand name Toyota, Nissan, Sanyo, Sony, Panasonic or JVC. Many manufactured products like cars and electronics were the preserves of the rich until the Japanese introduced the world to mass production. This way the cost of production for manufactured goods was significantly reduced and made affordable to all classes of people. In their feasibility study of the Promised Land, Moses required the twelve tribal leaders to investigate 'what the land is, whether it be fat or lean'. Expansive development is only possible with the availability of much land. This speaks of the potential capacity for increased productivity. Naturally, everyone involved in an organization would be delighted to see phenomenal growth.

Process

Process is the systematic way of achieving an objective. It is the series of changes that occur in the growth of an organism or the natural series of stages in any operation. When the right process is adopted, it results in a breakthrough. The wrong process is one that does not end up with a breakthrough.

The production of tangible goods is essential to sustain any economic environment. Farmers must produce food for consumption, engineers must produce technological equipment and carpenters must produce furniture. The endeavor to provide the tangible necessities of life results in the creation of material wealth. This process of creating material wealth entails adding value to tangible resources such as in mining, production, packaging etc. Manufacturing of semi-finished products, finished products or just re-packaging products of other producers are all options. A farming venture for instance, could be involved in the production of raw materials for the food industry or for domestic consumption. From land preparation through pest control and harvesting, a farmer would consider the best possible cultivation options, check the comparative advantages before making a choice. The process of production opted for, the plants and equipment required as well as the measures instituted, or quality standards must ultimately aim at both sustainability and excellence.

Just as God had a working relationship with Adam in the Garden of Eden, He wants to work with us to enhance our creativity and sustainability. In Isaiah 28:23-29 the scripture says: "Listen and hear my voice; pay attention and hear what I say. When a farmer plows for planting, does he plow continually? Does he keep on breaking up and harrowing the soil? When he has leveled the surface, does he not sow caraway and scatter cumin? Does he not plant wheat in its place, barley in its plot, and spelt in its field? His God instructs him and teaches him the right way. Caraway is not threshed with a sledge, nor is a cartwheel rolled over cumin; caraway is beaten out with a rod, and cumin with a stick. Grain must be ground to make bread; so one does not go on threshing it forever. Though he drives the wheels of his threshing cart over it, his horses do not grind it. All this also comes from the Lord Almighty, wonderful in counsel and magnificent in wisdom".

When you think of the human body and how it functions to process our respiration and metabolism to cause health and growth: isn't it wonderful? God taught Adam the first farmer, how to cultivate and harvest crops. Scripture testifies that He taught process to the first engineer, livestock farmer, musician, and the various professions. God gave Moses over six hundred laws which are basic principles to guide all manner of endeavoring.

Any process that tends to violate natural organic processes is usually classified as being scientifically artificial. Aiming at one hundred percent organic productivity process is an important burden for the believer. Though they may be advertised as cutting-edge technologically advanced methods, do not just assemble whatever processes your industry engages. History has proved repeatedly that artificial methods most often generate side effects that outweigh their advertised benefits. It is imperative that you get all the facts that pertain to available productivity processes, discern, and engage divine revelation in the choice of process for productivity. Your productivity process must never be contrary to God's way of doing things. This is the key to a sustainable breakthrough!

Tools of Creativity
Creativity is the key that unlocks the doors for progressive achievements. Jesus said: "The light of the

body is the eye: if therefore your eye be single, your whole body shall be full of light." Matthew 6:22. To enhance our innovative abilities, we must target our productivity at a particular niche, because specialization helps us remain on the cutting edge of our endeavors. Creativity is a function of the anointing and involves the ability to discern knowledge, engage the science of understanding and employ wisdom skillfully.

Discerning Knowledge

Effective management of information is a vital key for breakthroughs in this twenty-first century. Strategy thrives on the wings of information. Just as facts are available to all men through books and journals, truth is also available to believers either through the scriptures and by revelation. Every believer must cultivate the discipline of accessing these sources of information and discern which is appropriate for a given project or circumstance. Many people are guilty of mismanaging knowledge. Some do not give careful attention to valuable information they receive through dreams, visions, and prophesy. Others do not know what to do with such information. Furthermore, some misuse the information to their detriment. While facts are accessible to all, God gives the believer an advantage over the unbeliever by giving him truth as an additional and higher source of information. "But as it is written, Eye hath not seen, nor ear heard, neither have entered into the heart of man, the things which

God hath prepared for them that love him. But God hath revealed them unto us by his Spirit for the Spirit searches all things, yea, the deep things of God" 1 Corinthians 2:9-10. Our natural senses limit our sources of information to facts which have already been discovered and documented for our learning. Beyond facts are truths, which can be accessed through a personal relationship with the Lord Jesus Christ. History has shown that in every generation, certain known facts become obsolete and are replaced by new information. For instance, chemistry previously claimed that plastics did not possess properties for conducting electricity. Today, it has been discovered that certain polymers of plastic can conduct electricity. Whatever we know as facts today may be disproved tomorrow.

Unlike facts, truth does not change. Jesus is Truth and He is the same yesterday, today and forever. Truth is the foundation upon which the whole universe is established. Though we have facts to pursue our purposes, we still need truth to establish these purposes. God gives us truth by His Spirit dwelling in us. The Holy Spirit teaches us and reveals to us truth that is relevant to our purposes. "But the anointing which ye have received of him abides in you, and ye need not that any man teach you: but as the same anointing teaches you of all things, and is truth, and is no lie, and even as it hath taught you, you shall abide in him" 1 John 2:27. This anointing is a reference to the presence of the Holy Spirit in a believer's heart. The statement 'you need not that any man teach you' is a reference to an over-reliance upon facts discovered by men. The Holy Spirit endorses facts, which must be applied in every given circumstance of our pursuit of purpose. In addition to this, He also highlights truth that is relevant to the purpose at hand. Deep truths as well as important information which man has not yet discovered nor classified as facts are available to the believer through the anointing. Discerning knowledge is the ability to select the relevant facts and truths for application to a given process.

The Science of Understanding

Creativity involves the 'science of understanding'. Understanding represents two words – 'under' and 'stand'. The under-stand of a building is the foundation. Another meaning for understanding is 'insight'. It shows that understanding refers to the hidden principles behind any given knowledge. Understanding science therefore is the ability to research and discover the principles that govern known facts. For instance, why and how does a metal conduct electricity? It is called knowledge when you are aware that a given metal conducts electricity. However, when you know the reason why or how a given metal conducts electricity then you have understanding or insight. Understanding is a much deeper grasp of information. Many people have been able to acquire general knowledge about many things but only a few people have understanding about specific things. Those who possess understanding are those who pursue careers in specific disciplines to a high level. Such people spend much time studying a subject with a focus. The kind of focus you give your mind determines the amount of insight you acquire. With a single focus on a specific subject, you have the potential of gaining a great amount of understanding. However, 'if your eye is evil' or double, which refers to the absence of focus on a specific subject or project, then you will acquire no insight. It is always detrimental if what you consider as insight is false.

Understanding is the ability to research and discover the principles governing an accepted truth. When God speaks to us for the first time concerning a subject or process, that information serves as knowledge to us. It is our responsibility then to seek to understand this truth. God is never opposed to our quest for understanding. When we have insight into whatever He tells us to do, we can accomplish it better. Jesus taught in Matthew 7:7, "Ask, and it shall be given you; seek, and ye shall find: knock, and it shall be opened unto you". We ask for knowledge. Knowledge is the first dimension of revelation. We seek for understanding. Understanding is the second dimension of revelation. We knock for wisdom. Wisdom is the third dimension of revelation. God is interested in helping people attain all three dimensions of revelation. Indeed, these are the dimensions at which He desires to relate with us as humans.

"It is the glory of God to conceal a thing: but the honor of Kings is to search out a matter" Proverbs 25:2. God does not make all revelation of truth available to men. He expects prudent men to seek Him for the revelations they require. God deems men who seek Him for revelation as honorable. A man of understanding does not apply knowledge until he has sought the principle behind such knowledge. Many people allow unscriptural proverbial sayings of men to influence their decisions in the pursuit of purpose. This could be detrimental to your progress if the foundation for such an adage is not truth. Any good adage or proverb worth adopting must be strongly rooted in scripture.

Skillful In Wisdom

Finally, creativity involves being 'skillful in all wisdom'. Wisdom is the third level of revelation. Wisdom is the active aspect of revelation. To walk in wisdom is simply to walk in the insight that is acquired through knowledge. "I wisdom dwell with prudence and find out knowledge of witty inventions" Proverbs 8:12. Wisdom never takes a step unless it has established that this is true knowledge and full insight has been acquired. Notice the caliber of people who are appointed to head big corporations and ventures.

Usually, such people have acquired a high level of knowledge through education. Another prerequisite is the experience and understanding of the actual process of work. They are expected to employ knowledge and understanding as tools to harness the resources of the organization to accomplish expected results. They are entitled to higher salary remuneration, as compared with the ordinary worker who simply employs manpower to do their work. This might seem an injustice when you consider the amount of physical energy man-power-labor exert in work. However, when man-power-labor makes a mistake, it may easily be corrected without an overall effect upon the prosperity of the organization. On the other hand, a strategic mistake by higher-level management can cause the shutdown of the organization, hence, the disparity in remuneration.

Wisdom is the ability to employ knowledge and understanding to harness available physical resources to generate expected results. King David was distinguished as one who employed divine wisdom in leadership. Prior to his reign, there was a period when David was considered a rebel in Israel. He was hiding in the wilderness to escape from King Saul who sought to kill him. Some four hundred people had gathered around David, and he mobilized them into an army.

"Then they told David, saying, Behold, the Philistines fight against Keilah, and they rob the threshing floors.

Therefore David inquired of the LORD saying, Shall I go and smite these Philistines? And the LORD said unto David, Go, and smite the Philistines, and save Keilah. And David's men said unto him, Behold, we be afraid here in Judah: how much more then if we come to Keilah against the armies of the Philistines? Then David inquired of the LORD yet again. And the LORD answered him and said, Arise, go down to Keilah; for I will deliver the Philistines into thine hand. So David and his men went to Keilah, and fought with the Philistines and brought away their cattle, and smote them with a great slaughter. So David saved the inhabitants of Keilah." 1 Samuel 23:1-5

David received a report of an attack that the Philistines had launched on Keilah, an Israelite town. This information was a fact. He inquired from God to determine if it was His will to go and save the people of Keilah. God revealed that it was His will for David to go. This inquiry reveals that David was diligent in seeking to discern the fact of the situation as well as the truth of whether it was an assignment worth pursuing. David announced his decision to save Keilah to his army and their reaction was negative because such an expedition would expose their positions to King Saul. David did not abandon the mission but went the second time to inquire of God concerning this campaign against the Philistines and God assured David of victory. This second inquiry is evident of understanding. This comes into play when you subject knowledge acquired about an issue to a higher analysis. David and his men then moved to Keilah to engage the Philistines in battle after having received insight that victory was assured despite the dangerous circumstances. This is a display of wisdom that enabled David and his armies secure victory for the people of Keilah.

As believers, the anointing breeds authenticity for our mission through perseverance. A new service, product or process for productivity always requires the test of time to perfect. While an established enterprise may afford to lavish resources on their research and development department to bring new products to perfection, the new entrepreneur may not have access to such resources and must resort to perseverance. In the same way that a seed must undergo much pressure to produce oil, the fullness of the anointing is never manifested until we are subjected to many trials. The result is an authentic service or product that bears our DNA. This way, you are supernaturally distinguished from your competitors!

Productivity Pursuits

Naturally, the desire of a visionary is that the whole world should benefit from their endeavor. As much as this reflects positive aspiration, it seldom occurs where one can achieve such a vision in a short time. It becomes necessary to identify which aspects of the vision you can possibly achieve within the confines of your ability and available resources. Objectives are the various tasks into which a vision is divided. A big vision must be divided into smaller units, so that as you achieve these units you get closer to arriving at your ultimate vision. For instance, if you had a vision of building a very big confectionery, which is presently beyond your means, it is still possible to start by selling candies produced by other factories. Selling candies becomes a very good objective since it enables you capture a share of the candy market before you engage in its production. In addition, the experience gained in selling candies will provide investors with the confidence that they are not investing in a novice. To accomplish your vision easily, it must be divided into various objectives. Each of these objectives must satisfy the following criteria to be realistic.

Specific Objectives – This speak of a very well-defined endeavor that can be called by name, for example, training, planning, marketing, construction, or manufacturing. When an objective is not specific, it usually ends up as a white elephant. Such an uncompleted or underutilized endeavor is usually of little value to the owner. There is usually no focus and precious resources are lost whenever an objective is not clearly defined.

Measurable Objectives – It should be possible for you to assign a measure of money value, time, quality to the objective. Whenever an objective is measured, there is a natural drive for excellence and speedy achievement. When goals are unmeasured, people tend to become content with little achievement or procrastinate in their endeavors, which could ultimately frustrate the achievement of the goal.

Attainable Objectives – A good objective must be achievable. This means that one must carefully consider the availability of the resources necessary for the achievement of such an objective. Assumption and speculation must not be employed in the estimation of the cost of an objective.

Flexible Objectives – A good objective must be one that can be achieved through a variety of means. It is necessary to find all alternative ways of arriving at the objective. This provides you with other ways of pursuit once a given method fails.

Platform Objectives – A good objective must serve as the platform from which you can easily arrive at your next objective. To do this properly, it is vital to create a hierarchy of objectives that rise to the accomplishment of each goal. With the aid of good counsel and much diligence, re-arrange your objectives, prioritizing those that serve as a good platform for achieving subsequent ones.

CHAPTER
5

Market
Many Or Few People

I n almost every community of North America you will find Wal-Mart Stores, Target, Macys, and many other franchise enterprises conspicuously located. Making strategic use of the media, arts and entertainment, these companies have devised effective ways of drawing people to purchase their wares. Christmas week, Father's and Mother's Day, Memorial Day, weekends, and twenty-four hours a day people flock to these shops. North America has become the most strategic market for consumer goods, and producers from all over the world strive to penetrate this market.

In their study of the Promised Land, Moses required the twelve tribal leaders to observe if the people were 'few or many'. Only few people inhabit desert and arid areas. A great number of people usually cluster around a place where there is a great source of life. This is more likely to be around a water source. Jesus Christ is the living water that provides man with inspiration for life, salvation, healing, and miracles. His presence in the church today is the reason so many people flock to worship services every week. It is amazing how the politician, soldier, judge, technician, business tycoon, unemployed, homeless and people from all walks of life congregate under one roof to worship God.

The corporate world has recognized the large size of the church as a potential to be exploited. Today big companies owned by non-Christians consider churches, Christian conventions, crusades, and other religious programs as a target market. In certain cases, they enter into contractual agreements with Christian leaders to facilitate Christians as a market for their goods and services. In His day, Jesus Christ overturned the tables of traders and drove them out of the temple. These traders identified worshippers as a potential market for products and made a deal with the priests. The priests gave them a place in the temple to locate their businesses and so they turned the house of prayer into a den of thieves. The church is a place where Christians should find strength in every area of life. Unless there is an obvious advantage to believers, secular organizations should not be granted the opportunity to exploit the Body of Christ.

In all that we do both corporately and individually, we must be mindful of the kingdom design to facilitate wealth transfer in our favor. Baby steps that we all endeavor to take today, should ensure that future generations of believers have greater leverage and get to a better wealth place. "A good man leaves an inheritance to his children's children: and the wealth of the sinner is laid up for the just." Proverbs 13:22

The Marketer

The scriptures tell the story of Boaz, an Israelite who lived in Bethlehem-Judah. He was an ancestor of King David and was described as a mighty man of wealth. Boaz had a big farm cultivated with corn. During harvest he gladly employed the divine principle of gleaning. "When you reap the harvest of your land, you shall not wholly reap the corners of your field, nor shall you gather the gleanings of your harvest. And you shall not glean your vineyard, nor shall you gather every grape of your vineyard; you shall leave them for the poor and the stranger: I am the Lord your God." Leviticus 19:9-10

This principle was God's mandate for the rich to make provision for the poor, the successful to help those struggling in business, the professional to equip the disadvantaged and so on. Ruth was a poor Moabite who renounced her heathen ways to follow the God of Israel. She took advantage of this principle and gleaned the fields of Boaz. Among all the other gleaners, Boaz particularly noticed Ruth. He asked his staff about her and discovered she was the new convert. Ruth had distinguished herself as a convert with a good character. Boaz told Ruth not to glean elsewhere and provided abundant resources to meet her needs. Ruth met his criteria for a virtuous wife and eventually they got married and became ancestors of Jesus Christ.

By reason of salvation, the Christian carries the mark of divine favor. Furthermore, if we develop godly character, it becomes our goodwill. To secure the best business deals, courteous services, quality products and value for money, everyone looks out for goodwill. Whenever you walk into a store attended by salesmen, immediately you begin to seek and identify the one with a friendly disposition. If a particular salesperson meets your expectations, he or she becomes your preferred contact for services in this store.

Your integrity as a marketer is the foundation for success. Whatever you claim to be or claim to be able to do becomes a debt. As Christians we are endowed with favor, and it is our duty to leverage this goodwill in the marketplace. I was ministering for an entire week on spiritual emphasis at the Global Revival Bible School. On the last day as I headed back to my office after ministering, while driving on the highway, I heard the Holy Spirit whisper to "turn left" instead of a right turn towards my office. Immediately I obeyed and turned left, a car broke down in front of me. I parked my car and helped this fellow push his car from the middle of the highway to the shoulder. He requested to use my cell phone to call for the tow truck and when this was arranged, he asked for another favor. He was headed for an important meeting, and he needed a ride. I agreed and helped him to the meeting. When we arrived, I decided to wait for him to complete his transaction. When he was done, he introduced me to his host as the angel who helped him make the appointment. The host asked what I did for a living, and I told him of my business in marbles and granite. He asked if I had catalogues with me. In short, this was how I secured a contract worth one hundred and twenty thousand dollars!

While it is possible to obtain the same product or services from various business entities, the company that tends to attract and retain more customers is one that develops a humane approach to business. Today the customer service department has grown to become one of the most essential parts of a business. Some customer service departments are open twenty-four hours a day to answer questions and respond to complaints. As courteously as possible customer service personnel protect the integrity of the company by satisfying the needs of customers. Your testimonial would advertise you. You will be surprised at unexpected favor, which comes because of your goodwill that will be advertised in places beyond your reach.

Market Dynamics

God knew the importance of your purpose for which He released you to be a part of this generation. Society is always in need of righteous people who dispense favor. There is a market out there for what you produce. Furthermore, as Christians we are blessed with mighty wealthy relatives! There are many potential clients within the church who can become a reason for our success in pursuit of purpose. What the world calls 'coincidence' is spiritually referred to as 'divinely orchestrated'. It is possible you could be divinely connected to your miraculous breakthrough right in church. My wife Faith is a graphic artist by profession. We were standing in front of our church one day when a pastor pulled up and parked his car. He introduced himself as the head of a local church in the area. As we talked, it became apparent that he needed help to organize a major conference for a visiting evangelist. I volunteered to help. Through my new association with this pastor my wife secured her biggest single contract.

Market Analysis - "A poor man's field may produce abundant food but, lack of judgment sweeps it away" Proverbs 13:23. Our focused efforts coupled with insight of developments in our industry equip us to respond effectively to market challenges. Though a Christian involved in trading, manufacturing or services could have good stuff to offer to the market, an improper assessment of the market might result in poor business performance. We must design our enterprises to respond to the pace, pressures, and fluctuations of the business world. Competition, high customer expectation, cost pressures and market changes are all realities that we must constantly understand and work to overcome. The short-term trends of an industry usually delude many entrepreneurs into a state of complacency and as a result they fail to survive the test of time. You must regularly update yourself with information and understand the trends of your industry. Do not survive in business simply by trailing behind the blazing efforts of industry leaders. You must be responsive, that is, you must identify the needs of society in relation to your product and strive to be the best at meeting the need.

While in the process of conducting a survey in preparation to launch my commodities into a particular market, I secured my first deal. I met the owner of a company who was looking for alternative sources of supplies and he ordered from me. It is imperative that market analysis must be undertaken at the inception of any business. Market analysis is the evaluation of the market to ascertain the size and viability of the market. It is important to gauge the potential level at which people would patronize the product or service. By means of a questionnaire and possibly a product sample, conduct research to determine your potential customers. In your final analysis you must work out the size of the market and derive the magnitude of potential consumers. Determine the viability of the market, so you know the price at which you can sell to break-even and make profit. To achieve this, you must first ascertain the cost of production by adding total expenses to the value of the product. Second, you must cost your products in relation to the prices of your competitors. Ultimately you want to determine whether you can enter the market, sell to your potential customers, and make profit at the prices you have fixed for your products.

Market Intelligence - Jesus taught the essence of researching the strategic positioning of your competitors in the industry. "Or what King going to make war against another king, sitteth not down first, and consults whether he be able with ten thousand to meet him that cometh against him twenty thousand? Or else, while the other is yet a great way off, he sends ambassadors, and desires conditions of peace" Luke

14: 31-32. Since a business does not exist in isolation, it is important that you constantly evaluate the position of the business vis-a-vis others to remain competitive. By marketing intelligence, you constantly monitor the activities of your competitors to stay abreast with their new strategies. Such information makes you current with developments in the industry and enables you to formulate strategic plans to maintain and increase your market share. We must constantly analyze our strengths, weaknesses, opportunities, and threats in the business environment.

Market Segmentation - The market for any product could be so vast that if you do not identify a group of people with a common need and attempt to satisfy them, you may not breakthrough easily. Market segmentation is the concept of grouping people with a common need. By segmenting the market, we identify potential customers, know their demographics and needs. This way we can determine the right way to reach them. When you segment effectively, you direct all your resources and skill towards the selected segment. This is the principle known as targeting. It means 'aiming at something'. "The light of the body is the eye: If therefore thine eye be single, thy whole body shall be full of light. But if thine eye be evil, thy whole body shall be full of darkness. If therefore the light that is in thee be darkness, how great is that darkness" Matthew 6:22-23. Targeting could be described best as a hunter aiming to shoot at an animal. He focuses on the animal and nothing else. Targeting helps in specialization, the key to maximized results.

Marketing

Within every human being is the natural ability to understand tough problems and use new ideas to solve them. This becomes more apparent when we focus our endeavors in the arena of our divine potentials. In our pursuit of divine destiny, we are endowed supernaturally with the Spirit of knowledge, understanding and wisdom to advance in the face of all challenges. Creativity is the key when all known prospects for tackling a particular task become inadequate. It is essential to engage the mindset of God in view of difficult tasks. 'Is there anything too hard for the Lord?' Such attitude makes us pray to seek inspiration and revelation to advance. Remember that creativity is almost always the result of an attempt to meet a difficult need or overcome a challenge. Whatever problem you are diligent enough to solve by innovation sets you on the leading edge.

Businesses which have survived highly competitive markets are those which have operated with an emphasis on good reputation, among other things. Public opinion is an essential factor in the success and growth of every human oriented endeavor. This is the perception one has about a company and its products.

When a company's name, product or service is mentioned, those who are acquainted with the name immediately have an impression either of a good quality product and service or a bad one. It is important that you position your company and product positively in the consumer's mind.

"You shall not have in your bag differing weights, a heavy and a light. You shall not have in your house differing measures, a large and a small. You shall have a perfect and just weight, a perfect and just measure, that your days may be lengthened in the land which the Lord your God is giving you. For all who do such things, all who behave unrighteously, are an abomination to the Lord your God." Deuteronomy 25:13-16

In the past, people used standard metal weights to determine the value of their merchandise or grain. Certain dishonest businessmen were in the habit of cheating customers and would alter their weights when selling merchandise to unsuspecting buyers. Weights and measures were used to also determine the value of items like clothes or ropes. Dishonest businessmen would use substandard measurements to cheat prospective buyers. Today, many marketers disguise substandard products with marketing gimmicks. These practices violate the divine principles of marketing. As Christians we must be honest in what we say about our product when marketing it.

Promotion and Advertising - The advertising industry is worth billions of dollars because it is effectively the driving force for the sales of goods and services. It is an accepted fact today that it costs far more to advertise a product, than the cost of its development and production. The greatest burden of many enterprises is the need to raise huge sums for advertisement. Many small enterprises with good products may never evolve to become great enterprises because they cannot raise an advertising budget that effectively promotes them.

The body of Christ is an ecosystem that ought to mirror God's sovereign economy in heaven. As believers we must endeavor to develop our natural market by networking the hidden potentials of the feeble among us with our mighty relatives. Over three decades ago when I started pastoring, I dedicated babies to the Lord who today are practicing as medical professionals, engineers, successful entrepreneurs etc. I never once imagined that these babies would grow up to impact society so profoundly during my lifetime. In the story of Boaz and Ruth, it seemed as though Boaz was the only one with privileges by which to salvage Ruth until later it becomes evident that Ruth was heiress of an estate that significantly enlarged the wealth estate of Boaz.

Goodwill Advertising - "And when you reap the harvest of your land you shall not wholly reap the corners of your field, neither shall you gather the gleanings of your harvest. And you shall not glean your vineyard, neither shall you gather every grape of your vineyard: you shall leave them for the poor and stranger: I am the Lord your God" Leviticus 19:9-10.

The organic way to enter the market as a believer is through goodwill advertising. Certain companies, especially in the hospitality industry, offer complimentary or free service to potential customers as a strategic marketing tool. The divine marketing principle is that every organization should make provision for the needy in society. The public image of a business is positively enhanced when free stuff and food is regularly sent to orphanages, the homeless or retirement centers. Christian owned enterprises must have goals that mitigate the needs of the disadvantaged in society. Instead of employing traditionally expensive advertising, we must employ creative ways of promoting products and services while empowering society at the same time.

Forever 21 is a retail company that audaciously touts their goodwill efforts on their website. "At Forever 21, one of our core values is to encourage giving and to lend a helping hand to those who need it most. We are always finding ways to help our local communities and partner with charities of every scale. Over the years, we have carried products that has helped different organizations, such as Give to Love, Love to Give. We have also developed collaborative products with proceeds benefiting charitable organizations. A current exciting project is with Project Level to develop a collaborative line of products. Project Level is an amazing non-profit organization which nurtures the creative needs of at-risk and underserved inner-city youth in the San Francisco Bay area. When we partner with an organization on a specific collection, a portion of the proceeds is donated to the designated charity. We continue to support Boys & Girls Clubs and Girls Inc. with significant donations. At home, Forever 21 is an avid and consistent supporter of the local community near its corporate headquarters in Los Angeles. For example, the company had funded college scholarships and supported summer camp opportunities for local youth in the neighborhood and continues to support the Los Angeles Police Department's Hollenbeck PAL Program.

Hobby Lobby is another retail enterprise that has boldly published their participation in goodwill efforts on their website. "Hobby Lobby gives a 10 percent in-store discount to churches, schools, and national charitable organizations for purchases made with an organizational check or credit card."

The Marketing Mix – This is how you combine various media to effectively reach your target market:

Syndicated Radio and Television Programs – Informative programs that provide basic education serve as a vital way of assisting the public in overcoming ignorance. At the same time this leads people to know where they can obtain such products and services.

Church Business Development Seminars – Seminars conducted within churches to provide industry-specific information and free counseling is a strategic way of developing acquaintance with potential clients.

Business Referral – To keep wealth within the Body of Christ, we should always recommend tested services from Christians to others.

Trade Shows – Participation in Christian trade shows provides a forum for display of new products, an opportunity to offer discounts to clients as well as a platform for networking.

Concert Sponsorships – Christian entertainers would achieve a greater level of impact through a collaborative effort with Christian businesses. This way a three-fold benefit is derived as our social needs would be met, Christian entertainers would advance, and businesses would be promoted.

Sports Sponsorships – Sports sponsorship also produces a three-fold benefit that enhances our social lives, the career of our sports men and as well businesses get promoted.

Print Media Features – Christian professionals should provide general counsel through articles in magazines. Readers get to know how such professionals or businesses have positioned themselves to meet their needs.

Internet Marketing – With almost everyone having a technological gadget such as a cellphone, online marketing has become an effective marketing media which we must utilize to make our businesses accessible to society.

Hexagon Quadrilateral

Hexagon Quadrilateral

CHAPTER
6

Finance
Strongholds Or Tents

T hrough a unique system of banking that facilitates customers with secret accounts, Switzerland has remained the greatest banking center of the world for years. Financial resources from all over the world flow to this banking haven, providing a strong foundation for the Swiss economy. In their study of the Promised Land, Moses mandated the twelve tribal leaders to look out for 'what cities they be that they dwell in, whether in tents, or in strongholds'. Treasures of wealth will not be very secure in tents. Wherever treasures of wealth are available, strongholds are built to protect them.

The world of business and work is very complex, involving activities of people from various backgrounds. The forces of intellectualism, manipulation, and greed as well as spiritual forces of evil and good all come into play. Government policies, decisions of corporations and financial institutions as well as supply and demand factors also influence the fate of all people involved in work. These factors create an extremely competitive environment in which Christians must not only survive but also take the lead. I have often been confronted by Christians who say 'I have been faithful in my tithing and offerings for many years now, yet I don't seem to be making any headway financially'. I usually tell such people the story about the biscuit-making machine that required various ingredients such as flour, milk, sugar and flavor at the input end to turn out delicious biscuits. One day, the confectioner fed the machine with only flour expecting to receive biscuits. Unfortunately, the output was flour dust! In my research of the scriptural principles of financial prosperity I discovered that tithing, offerings and almsgiving constituted approximately thirty percent of what it took for a man to prosper financially. Fortunately, Christians across the world are conversant with these three principles. The sad aspect is that most Christians do not know the remaining requirements for prosperity.

Despite the awesome presence of God that produces salvation, healing and deliverance in the local church, many Christians today are poor and financially frustrated. Over the years I have partnered with notable evangelists involved in massive soul winning crusades across the world and observed that many of the saved souls drifted back to the world of sin because of poverty. They would often compromise their faith to secure finances for their basic needs. Though we began to conduct financial empowerment sessions to enlighten believers on the need for giving in order to increase financially, it was apparent that the local church also had a role to play as prescribed by the scriptures. The apostles, prophets, evangelists, pastors and teachers of today's church have equipped Christians to attain spiritual and moral freedom. The stage is set for the next level of blessing that is coming to the body of Christ. Prophetically speaking, I am convicted that deacons and elders of the local church would position Christians to inherit the wealth of the wicked.

On the day of Pentecost, the disciples of Jesus experienced the baptism of the Holy Spirit, and the New Testament church was born. Three thousand souls were won to Christ on this day. They instituted regular fellowship to facilitate the spiritual, moral, and financial wellbeing of every member. "And the multitude of them that believed were of one heart and of one soul: neither said any of them that ought of the things which he possessed was his own; but they had all things in common. And with great power gave the apostles witness of the resurrection of the Lord Jesus: and great grace was upon them all. Neither was there any among them that lacked: for as many as were possessors of lands or houses sold them, and brought the prices of things that were sold, And laid them down at the apostles feet: and distribution was made unto every man according as he had need. And Joses, who by the apostles was surnamed Barnabas, which is being interpreted The son of consolation, a Levite, and of the country of Cyprus, Having land, sold it, and brought the money, and laid it at the apostles' feet" Acts 4:32-37. The early church was able to meet the needs of her members and so prosperity abounded. This was achieved through a pooling of resources, which were administered in such a way as to meet the needs of the people. The institution of the church ensured the prosperity of every member by catering for spiritual, moral and financial needs. However, in most churches today the spiritual and moral wellbeing of members is taken care of, but the church has shied away from the foundations that brought financial freedom to Christians.

Sources of Financing

The availability of reliable sources of financing is an essential factor for any endeavor to prosper. All economic activity requires some form of financing.

Finance can be raised through the liquidation of inheritance, personal savings, equity from friends and relatives, business credit and loans from financial institutions.

Liquidation of Assets - "Again, the kingdom of heaven is like treasure hidden in a field, which a man found and hid; and for joy over it he goes and sells all that he has and buys that field. "Again, the kingdom of heaven is like a merchant seeking beautiful pearls, who, when he had found one pearl of great price, went and sold all that he had and bought it." Matthew 13:44-46.

Jesus Christ taught the need for men to gravitate their resources towards their divine financial purpose once they discovered it. With two parables, Jesus confirms that a man's financial purpose is a very valuable treasure. Every entrepreneur seeks to pursue the most lucrative investment. When he discovers which business represents his divine potential, he should wisely disinvest from all other businesses and invest into his divine destiny. Ultimately it is the pursuit of your divine destiny that would ensure that every blessing of God assigned for you as a believer would materialize. Blessings of success and prosperity are assured for every believer conducting themselves according to the purposes of God. Invest a significant portion of your resources into the pursuit of your divine purpose and position yourself to reap God's blessings.

Personal Savings - "When you sit down to eat with a ruler, consider carefully what is before you; and put a knife to your throat if you are a man given to appetite. Do not desire his delicacies, for they are deceptive food." Proverbs 23:1-3

Our ability to save depends on how we spend our income. If you allocate all your earnings towards meeting domestic needs, then you are sure to have nothing left to invest. If you are employed and earn a regular income, then you must consider yourself privileged to dine with the king. Your income provides finances to meet your needs. Have you thought of what could happen if you lost this privilege of earning a regular income? In fact, you could lose this job if the king decides to deny you this privilege. The wise thing to do in view of this uncertainty, is to conduct yourself as though you did not have a job at all. It is not wise to settle into lavish domestic comfort if you are employed by someone else and cannot absolutely guarantee the future of this job. A substantial portion of your income from your current job must be channeled into an investment or savings. These funds should be reserved for ultimate investment into one's financial purpose.

Equity - "My son, if you become surety for your friend, If you have shaken hands in pledge for a stranger, You are snared by the words of your mouth; You are taken by the words of your mouth. So do this, my son, and deliver yourself; For you have come into the hand of your friend: Go and humble yourself; Plead with your friend. Give no sleep to your eyes, Nor slumber to your eyelids. Deliver yourself like a gazelle from the hand of the hunter, And like a bird from the hand of the fowler." Proverbs 6: 1-5.

Equity capital is the name given to funds, which usually come from the promoters of the company, their family, relatives, friends, and other people. Since most new businesses generally do not make profits immediately, they do not attract funds from the big financial institutions, hence, these kinds of funds are more accessible. It is wise to always begin a venture with your personal resources and establish a track record. Investors would be quick to invest into a business if they have evidence of its profit potential. In any case, such investors must be Christians if they are to become co-owners of your business. Do not be hasty to entertain investment capital with unbelievers because it seems to hold promise of being a quicker way to succeed. It is important that you prayerfully discern all potential investors.

To act as surety for a friend is to sign as a guarantor to pay his debt in case he does not. To 'strike hands with a stranger' is to enter into partnership or agreement with an unbeliever. Such commitment is a potential trap which could be detrimental to you. The most sensible thing to do is to go immediately to this fellow and tactfully disengage yourself from your previous commitment. Do not procrastinate on this matter. Take a cue from the deer or the bird that is evading death at the hands of hunters. Partnership with an unbeliever is detrimental to your divine destiny. Come out of it now and separate yourself. No matter how much it costs you today, it will eventually save your financial destiny from the schemes of the enemy.

"You shall not plow with an ox and a donkey together." Deuteronomy 22:10.

This is where two or more people of different value systems partner as the founders of an enterprise. "Do not be unequally yoked together with unbelievers. For what fellowship has righteousness with lawlessness? And what communion has light with darkness? And what accord has Christ with Belial? Or what part has a believer with an unbeliever? And what agreement has the temple of God with idols? For you are the temple of the living God. As God has said: "I will dwell in them and walk among them. I will be their God, and they shall be My people." Therefore "Come out from among them and be separate, says the Lord. Do not touch what is unclean, And I will receive you." "I will be a Father to you, and you shall be My sons and daughters, Says the Lord Almighty." 2 Corinthians 6:14-18

For the Christian, every strategic alliance must conform to the plowing principle. Plowing means to break up the soil. When an ox and a donkey are yoked together for plowing, it indicates two different animals joined to accomplish work. Even though an ox may look very much like a donkey, the bone structure of an ox, its natural physical disposition and ability is entirely different. If you yoked these two animals together to work, you would be placing one of the animals in a disadvantaged position. The animal whose natural design is more formidable would rest the burden of the yoke on the other. A clearer example would be to place a long bar on the heads of two men to carry, one tall man and the other short. The tall man will naturally balance the bar, so it rests strongly on the head of the short man.

The believer engages himself in work or business in pursuit of divine purpose. The plowing principle does not permit him to enter partnership with an unbeliever to fulfill this conviction. The believer is a temple in which God dwells as a habitation while the unbeliever is a temple of devils. The Greek root for the word fellowship is 'metoche', which means intercourse or intimate participation. In decision-making, you consult the Spirit of God as a believer, while the unbeliever draws from his carnal mind. Light does not reveal itself alongside darkness. Either light would prevail over darkness or vice versa. These are two opposing forces that are contrary to one another. If they form an association, which is also the legal term for a company, there will be confusion. Both darkness and light would complain about attempts of one party to subvert and overshadow the other. The light of God's Word in a believer cannot produce any good fruit in partnership with schemes of darkness. Christ is the Head of the believer. He is his source of influence while Satan is the source of influence for the unbeliever. The believer's profit in business emanates from Christ who provides a harvest for him, as a result of his faithful submission to divine convictions and principles of prosperity. When God blesses the believer, then the unbeliever with whom he is unequally yoked in partnership will automatically participate in the harvest.

Some Christians enter partnership with an unbeliever with the excuse that perhaps the unbeliever is in a particularly advantaged position to promote growth of their enterprise. This should not be an excuse because whenever God gives you a seed of conviction, he knows perfectly well your current position in life and what you possess both potentially and physically. God can bring the believer to the place of fulfillment and prosperity without the partnership of an unbeliever.

Whenever we have opportunity to invest or enter into collaborative agreements, we must watch out and avoid unequal yoking. The trend for investment into securities has changed dramatically since it has become obvious that ordinary shares are so much subject to human manipulation. In the US alone over two hundred Stock Exchange malpractice cases occur annually. This relatively high level of malpractice is evidence that investment into ordinary shares may not always be secure, despite the many regulations that govern the trading of stocks and the financial operations of Public Limited Liability Companies. To insulate your finances from the inevitabilities of stocks, many financial planners tend to suggest a diversification of investments. This way, you invest a certain percentage of your money into ordinary shares and the rest into bonds and treasury bills.

If done without conviction, investing into the stocks of a secular company may be a form of unequal yoking. The purchase of ordinary shares automatically makes the investor a joint owner of this company. However, if we are specifically convicted by the Holy Spirit to invest in a particular secular stock, it may be the strategic way of buying out the other stakeholders to secure primary ownership.

Investment securities like bonds and treasury bills are classified as loans to corporations and the government respectively. They usually have a fixed rate of return and do not contravene the scriptures so Christians can comfortably invest in this direction.

Loans - Banks and financial institutions offer loans to prospective entrepreneurs. Usually, the financial institutions require some form of collateral security as a guarantee for the loan. Interest would be charged at a rate that reflects the risk level of the venture as well as the current market rate. In addition, financial institutions require a comprehensive business plan backed by a strong performance record. This means that they may not be willing to lend money to a start-up entrepreneur. Before you attempt to secure a loan from any financial institution, you should invest your own resources to get the business started and running for some time. When you have established a track record of success, financial institutions may then lend you money if you meet all the set criteria.

Credit Facilities - Some companies offer credit terms of business to clients based upon specified conditions. This may be a better alternative to loans, since interest charged on goods sold on credit may be lower. A client of mine who had received approval for a bank loan for his business approached me for management counsel. After carefully quizzing him about his operations and the conditions of this loan, I advised him against accessing this money. Instead, I recommended credit purchasing as well as contract sales. This strategy annulled the need for the bank loan. The principal advantage was that he avoided the payment of high interest.

Christian Wealth System

The church constitutes three groups of people – the leadership, those who have abundant resources and those who lack resources. With a proper administration, this triangle has the potential to eradicate poverty from the local church. We identify these three groups of people when Jesus facilitated the miraculous multiplication of five loaves and two fishes. The first group comprised of Jesus and the apostles, the second group was the little boy with five loaves and two fishes, while the third group was a hungry crowd of over five thousand people. The apostles of the New Testament Church invoked this strategy to overcome the financial challenges of the members of the Church.

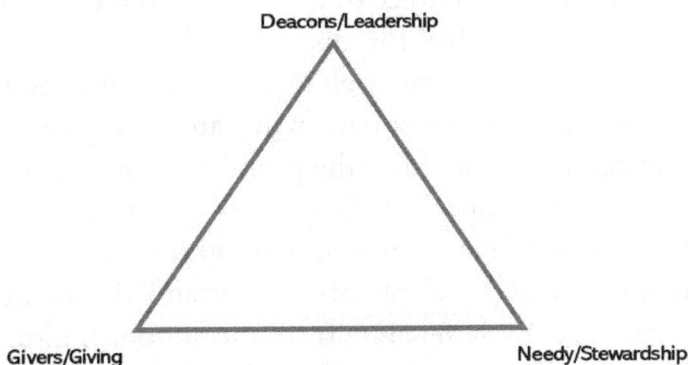

Deacons/Leadership

Givers/Giving   Needy/Stewardship

The Deacons – Leadership: On the day of Pentecost, the New Testament church was born, and the apostles availed themselves as a channel of God to alleviate the spiritual, moral and financial needs of the people. To effectively manage the financial needs of the membership, seven deacons were appointed. Though today's local church has instituted the office of the deacon, in most cases deacons function differently from the original purpose. Most deacons are responsible for spiritual and moral needs such as soul winning, ushering, marriage counseling, security, prayer and so on. Very little attention is usually given to the financial needs of members. The financial welfare needs of the church are enormous and take a lot of courage to tackle. Yet this is the key to a greater level of commitment and growth for the local church. The criteria for selecting deacons were that these seven men had distinguished themselves as honest, full of the Holy Spirit and wisdom. The local church must uphold these qualifications in its choice of deacons for three reasons. Firstly, it is possible for dishonest deacons to take undue advantage of this welfare program for personal gain. Second, professionals who are not prayerful would certainly jeopardize the purpose of this program with worldly counsel. Thirdly, if those selected lack entrepreneurial experience the program could easily end up as a white elephant. The wealth deployment program is entirely separate from the administration of tithes and offerings, which is outside the scope of this book. The financial welfare of members may at best be considered as the administration of alms.

Compassion: The burden to meet a need of mankind is the key to experiencing the miraculous. Such desire to meet the needs of others is known as compassion. It refers to inward affection and sympathy. It is the nature of God inherent in mankind. Everyone potentially possesses compassion that translates into a burden for his fellow men. God created man to make a definite impact upon his generation by alleviating the circumstances of other men and to make this world a better place to live. As leader of the ministry, Jesus knew how every need would be taken care of. "And Jesus, when he came out, saw many people, and was moved with compassion toward them, because they were as sheep not having a shepherd: and he began to teach them many things. And when the day was now far spent, his disciples came unto him, and said, This is a desert place, and now the time is far passed: Send them away, that they may go into the country round about, and into the villages, and buy themselves bread: for they have nothing to eat. He answered and said unto them, Give ye them to eat. And they say unto him, Shall we go and buy two hundred pennyworth of bread, and give them to eat? He saith unto them, How many loaves have ye? go and see. And when they knew, they say, five, and two fishes. And he commanded them to make all sit down by companies upon the green grass. And they sat down in ranks, by hundreds, and by fifties.

And when he had taken the five loaves and the two fishes he looked up to heaven, and blessed, and brake the loaves, and gave them to his disciples to set before them: and the two fishes divided he among them all. And they did all eat, and were filled. And they took up twelve baskets full of the fragments, and of the fishes. And they that did eat of the loaves were about five thousand men" Mark 6:34-44. The need to feed over five thousand people who gathered to listen to Jesus was certainly a great challenge. The only available food was five loaves of bread and two fishes. With the twelve disciples, Jesus established his management team. Making use of divine strategies, He organized the people and administered the resources. When Jesus reached out to ameliorate the circumstances of the people, He had the blueprint for the miraculous multiplication of available resources to meet their needs. Jesus recognized that the root cause of the challenges of these people was that of leadership. He began to teach them how to be repositioned for victory in their life pursuits. After a whole day of teaching, it was time to demonstrate the efficacy of the principles of God's word. The process he engaged for the miraculous multiplication of available resources is the key to wealth deployment in the local Church.

The Welfare Plan: Our society today is composed of more financially frustrated people than prosperous people. The factors responsible for such a trend have been diagnosed from various perspectives. Some

124

schools of thought hold the view that an uneven distribution of the world's resources of wealth is responsible. Others believe that the lack of opportunities in certain communities is an essential factor. Still some also believe supernatural forces like curses have a role to play. To some extent, such assertions may be right but not absolute. It is on record that even where poor people were allocated with resources, opportunities were placed at the disposal of the disadvantaged and spiritual deliverance administered for the oppressed, only a small fraction of these people succeeded, and prospered. Those who are unable to harness their resources, opportunities and spiritual liberty to better their lot most likely operate in ways contrary to divine principles. "By wisdom is a house built, and through understanding it is established; through knowledge its rooms are filled with rare and beautiful treasures" Proverbs 24:3-4. Knowledge, understanding, and wisdom are three principal qualifications required to achieve a goal. Knowledge means acquaintance with principles, truths, facts and information. It can be described as resources or materials that can be used for building a house. Understanding is insight. It is one's grasp of how to effectively use resources to achieve goals. Wisdom is the power to properly administer one's ways. It is the practical utilization of resources based on insight to achieve goals. "But the noble man makes noble plans, and by noble deeds he stands" Isaiah 32:8. A noble man is simply one who has resolved to conduct himself within the boundaries of knowledge, understanding and wisdom. Based upon the principles of knowledge, understanding and wisdom the noble man carefully formulates a plan. "The plans of the diligent lead to profit, as surely as haste leads to poverty" Proverbs 21:50. Failure, poverty and frustration can be attributed often to the lack of proper planning. Planning sometimes requires more investment of time and financial resources than the actual work the plan seeks to accomplish. To arrive at a feasible and viable plan, much consultation is necessary. "Plans fail for lack of counsel, but with many advisers they succeed" Proverbs 15:22. Books, journals, libraries, trade associations, seminars and workshops are sources of counsel. Professionally, it is wise to engage consultants especially when you intend to invest huge sums of money into a venture. A plan is a document that clearly defines your purpose, vision and objectives. It reveals how you determined your vision, why it would succeed, how you intend to pursue it as well as what resources it would require. The benefits of a carefully formulated master plan for the financial welfare of the members in the local church are twofold. First, it gives every member a clear understanding of the vision to ameliorate poverty. Secondly, it establishes the strategy for accomplishing goals which gives members of the local Church the confidence to provide resources necessary to make the program succeed.

Executing The Welfare Plan:

126

a) Stocktaking –Jesus displayed prudence by taking stock of all material assets, appraising the human resource and coordinating the collated information for reallocation of resources. Prudence is to optimize resources and employ multiple solutions to advance our course. To generate increase, we do not always have to necessarily engage more resources. Most often, it simply takes a good mix of existing resources, human resource potentials and entrepreneurial skill to generate more output. Our human and material resources are the seed capital that is divinely provided to facilitate our desired miracle. Making use of a questionnaire, the deacons should assist everyone in the local church to develop a business and professional profile. An 'Economic Empowerment Fund' must be established and a program to raise funds put in place. Everyone should be encouraged to contribute on a regular basis. Out of the tithes given by members, the local church must regularly seed the Economic Empowerment Fund. The business owners should be encouraged to pledge meaningful commitments, as this fund may be a source of financing in time of need. All salary earners in the church must also pledge to contribute on a regular basis so that whenever they decide to start their own business the fund becomes a source of financing.

b) Set Goals– He commanded that the people be organized into groups of hundreds and fifties. When problems are broken down into various tasks, it becomes easy to accomplish them. Each of the twelve disciples was responsible for a particular group that reflected his area of expertise. Similarly, every deacon must be assigned to a specific economic segment. For instance, all engineers should be assigned a deacon who is an engineer by profession. Each group must set goals to advance their group while meeting needs of the other economic groups. Brainstorming sessions to aid strategic planning, mentoring programs and job creation are typical goals each group must fulfill. Overall, one of the deacons responsible for economic empowerment must be designated as Economic Empowerment Officer to coordinate economic empowerment in the Church.

c) Worship – He blessed God for the available resources. Tithing and offerings represent our thanksgiving and worship which invokes divine revelation for prosperity. To eradicate poverty from among believers, everyone in the local church must be encouraged to tithe. Whoever does not tithe becomes a loophole for the devil to steal and destroy. At least ten percent of the funds raised for the Economic Empowerment Fund must be channeled to feed the hungry, care for the homeless and destitute.

d) Administer Resources – Whenever resources are administered within the framework of scriptural principles, divine purposes, godly planning and covenant pursuit, the result is multiplication! Jesus gave the available resources to the disciples who in turn administered it among the people. The disciples administered the resources in pursuit of the goals they set for their groups. If the goal of each group focuses on meeting their own needs as well as needs of other economic segments, the cycle of wealth generation is orchestrated. From the Economic Empowerment Fund, interest free loans should be disbursed to businesses in need of financing. If the Fund cannot facilitate the needs of a particular business, the deacons should identify strategic investors within the local church who would provide equity capital. This way the investors become joint owners of the venture. The business requiring such financing must be tasked to generate a comprehensive business plan. It is incumbent upon the leaders of the program to carefully monitor all synergistic relationships it promotes within the local church. Furthermore, to ensure that Christians employ the principles that would ascertain success in business pursuit, economic empowerment sessions should be conducted regularly to highlight divine principles and aid the development of entrepreneurial skills. Exhibitions and networking programs would serve as a market forum and facilitate synergies.

The Givers – Giving: The little boy with five loaves and two fishes surrendered his resources to the apostles. This humble fellow willingly gave his lunch as a seed that resulted in the miraculous feeding of over five thousand people. Givers in the New Testament church facilitated the seed capital of the Wealth Deployment Program. They pledged resources, as they were capable of fulfilling. "For as many as were possessors of lands or houses sold them, and brought the prices of things that were sold, And laid them down at the apostles feet: and distribution was made unto every man according as he had need. And Joses, who by the apostles was surnamed Barnabas, which is being interpreted The son of consolation, a Levite, and of the country of Cyprus, Having land, sold it, and brought the money, and laid it at the apostles' feet" Acts 4:32-37. Owners of properties liquidated their pledged assets and gave the money into the welfare purse. This way the needs of everyone in the church were taken care of. Ananias and Saphira, a dishonest couple who attempted to deal fraudulently with leadership, invoked the wrath of divine judgement and died!

Giving is a privilege God accords us to enable us enter into His favor of blessings. "Cast your bread upon the waters and you shalt find it after many days. Give a portion to seven, and also to eight; for you do not know what evil shall be upon the earth. In the morning sow your seed, and in the evening withhold not your hand: for you know not, which will prosper, either this or that, or whether they both shall be alike good" Ecclesiastics 11:1,2,6. To cast your bread upon the waters is the act of placing your comfort and convenience today at God's disposal. If you invest out of your material and financial comfort to fulfill what God requires of you today, you will reap your reward at some point in the future. Whenever the Holy Spirit prompts you to give to meet a specific need, be quick to obey. Also, do not only limit yourself to the Holy Spirit's conviction. 'Give a portion to eight' is to give to the poor and needy. Never get tired or fed up with giving. The more you give, you guarantee yourself of greater future harvests. Whatever you give, God will cause men to bring back to you in good measure, pressed down, shaken together and running over.

To demonstrate miraculous multiplication, Jesus gave the broken loaves to the disciples who in turn gave them to the people. Everyone ate until they were satisfied, and the leftovers filled twelve baskets. Giving was the principle Jesus applied here. In this miracle of multiplication, we first see a little boy who is willing to give his resource to Jesus to meet the needs of a very great crowd. Jesus is willing to give this blessed resource to the disciples. The disciples then give their apportioned resources to the people. The people eat and give the leftovers to the disciples again. There is a cycle of giving here which is unending.

"There is that scatters, and yet increases: and there is that withholds more than is meet, but it tends to poverty. The liberal soul shall be made fat: and he that waters shall be watered also himself. He that withholds corn, the people shall curse him: but blessing shall be upon the head of him that sells it" Proverbs 11:24-26.

Giving is the definite key to experience increase. Every man has been positioned by God to become a channel for another's blessings. Whatever you have was made possible because you received from someone. "And what have you that thou did not receive? Now if you did receive it, why do you glory, as if you had not received it?" 1 Corinthians 4:7. Whenever any man breaks the cycle of supply by refusing to give, he brings upon himself curses that result in poverty. The cycle of giving ensures that wealth is distributed to everyone in need. This is a divine principle which men must honor to stay in prosperity. By divine supernatural means the giver experiences a harvest of good measure, pressed down, shaken together and running over (Luke 6:38). If you keep giving, you keep receiving. Failure to give is indicative that you do not believe in the God who is able to supply all your needs according to His riches in glory. As we saw earlier, everyone in the cycle, from the little child to Jesus, the disciples and the crowd were all willing givers, hence, the manifestation of miraculous multiplication. As givers in the triangle of welfare administration, God will bless our pursuits and channel to us greater resources.

The Needy – Stewardship: Prosperity is not reserved for the rich but rather for everyone who

would recognize that his or her resources could be harnessed for an investment. The principle of using what you have, to get what you need is the key to financial freedom and success in the pursuit of divine purpose. This is demonstrated in 2 Kings 4:1-7 when Elisha asked the poor indebted widow who cried to him for help what resources she had available. The pot of oil was enough to change her circumstances once she was told she could trade it with her neighbors. God gives everyone resources according to his or her divine purpose and assignment.

In the parable of the talents, Jesus taught the essence of working with our available resources. "For the kingdom of heaven is as a man traveling into a far country, who called his own servants, and delivered unto them his goods. And unto one he gave five talents, to another two, and to another one; to every man according to his several ability; and straightway took his journey. Then he that had received the five talents went and traded with the same, and made them other five talents. And likewise he that that received two, he also gained other two. But he that had received one went and digged in the earth, and hid his lord's money, After a long time the lord of those servants cometh, and reckoneth with them" Matthew 25:14-19. The master in the scripture above is symbolic of God while his servants represent His children. This master was traveling on a long journey, which is symbolic of the number of years we must live here on earth. God has endowed everybody with various abilities and provided resources to enable us to pursue our purpose. Personal abilities include our talents and potentials. Though a student may not excel in mathematics he could excel in literature and produce excellent films for entertainment. A mathematician pays money to watch the movie and acknowledges it as a brilliant work of art. God has given every one of us great gifts. For that reason, we must not look down or envy another's talents. The servants in this scripture were allocated financial resources based upon their individual gifts and abilities. A man who desires to be involved in manufacturing needs to be given a larger sum of money for investment capital as compared to an accountant whose ambition is to rise as an employee in government service to become the head of treasury. If this potential manufacturer inherits a huge sum of money in life, it is God's provision of capital for his business. This should not arouse jealousy in the accountant since he does not need such a huge sum but rather a lower but consistent remuneration every month. As a student in high school, I realized that the money I was given per semester was substantial. My God ordained purpose in life, necessitated that money came to me at that early age and I invested my resources into business. Today I share many of my business experiences as I teach Christians about finance and business. This did not make me better than my colleagues who did not have such money at the time. Today, those who are judicious with their resources are equally prospering. The servants who were given five and two talents invested them and gained five and two more respectively. Their yield was one hundred percent. This indicates maximum return. If you judiciously invest every resource that God has given to you, you have the potential to reap one hundred percent returns. The seamstress, mechanic, carpenter and mason all have the potential to make a hundred percent return.

When God called me into business several years ago, the first thing He told me was to convert my bedroom into an office. This was my capital contribution to the business. My bedroom was strategically located at the entrance of the house and was ideal for an office. I shared my brother's bedroom with him, while my bedroom became an asset for a business that became prosperous. The servant with the one talent was the only one who did not invest but dug a hole and hid it. He described his master as a wicked man who wanted to harvest where he had not sown. This assertion was false since the master made available to him, financial resource.

God values everything He has given to men. Yet many people do not value their resources when it looks little in comparison to others. The servant with five talents did not use the talent to satisfy his lustful desires. Rather, he invested all and gained one hundred percent profit. Many complain and make excuses for not investing. Such people can be compared to that servant who was given one talent but buried it, blaming other people for his predicament. This servant did not invest because he did not value his resource. God has given everyone resources to make it in life. It is important that you take stock of these resources, mobilize them, and invest diligently into your financial destiny.

The master rewarded his servants who made an investment because of their faithfulness. God never entrusts you with many things until you have been faithful with few things. Faithfulness starts when you harness your resources and invest. Though you are employed as a messenger in an organization, aspire to become the managing director, according to God's promises. Pursue your responsibilities as a good manager of time, information and money. Your faithfulness as a messenger will earn you the favor to rise the ranks until you attain the position of a managing director. "Moreover it is required in stewards, that a man be found faithful." 1 Corinthians 4:2. Steward is an historical word for manager. Whenever God entrusts resources to anyone, God requires that person to whom He has entrusted resources such as time, information, money, goods, education and so on, be found faithful. As we harness all resources available to us for prudent investment into our divine purposes, we qualify for divinely orchestrated success and prosperity.

Financial Management

Managing the funds of an enterprise is one area where many have failed and as a result become bankrupt. The reasons for such failure range from a lack of clearly defined purpose for the various forms of funds available to the organization and consequent mismanagement. Very often when people are quizzed about why their enterprises are not flourishing, the answer is the absence of sufficient capital. While this may be true for some, it is on record that most people who receive loans also end up bankrupt. As much as possible, it is more expedient to exhaust all strategies for accomplishing objectives before accessing loans. Even when it becomes unavoidable, the purpose for this loan must be clearly defined as well as the income generating potential.

The Horizontal Table of Objectives

Goal Description	Desired Quantity	Quantity Available	Income Generation Potential
Trucks	5 ($250,000)	$250,000	40%
(B)Brick Machines	20 ($10,000)	-	60%
(C) Acres of Land	5 ($5,000)	-	70%
(D) Staff	30 ($30,000)	5 ($5,000)	80%
(E)Working Capital	$5,000	-	100%
Total	$300,000	$255,000	0%

This kind of table is recommended in situations where you have one of your main objectives already met. For instance, in a scenario where you possess all five trucks you need for a brick factory, you would be able to achieve the remaining objectives horizontally. In this table, the objectives are arranged according to the income generating potential of what we possess. The trucks can be operated as transporters of sand to supply other brick factories. The income generated should be invested in the next objective, which can also generate income and at the same time bring you closer to your vision of a brick factory. The objectives of the horizontal table are measured individually according to their income generating potentials. The five trucks represent the first objective that has the greatest income generating potential of forty percent. The second, third, fourth and fifth objectives are arranged according to how closer they bring us to achieve one hundred percent. At hundred percent capitalization our bricks factory worth three hundred thousand dollars is fully operational. You realize that it is possible to accomplish the vision of a bricks factory, not by securing a loan of three hundred thousand dollars at the onset of the mission. This places undue stress on the enterprise to perform at a level at which one may not be ready to be fully operational to service such a huge debt. Entering an industry in a tactful way ensures that the necessary operational experience as well as clientele building is accomplished with the least amount of stress.

The Vertical Table of Objectives

Goal	Desired Qty	Min. Qty Required	Substitute	Available Asset
(A) Machines	20 ($10,000)	1 ($500)	Manual Machine ($150)	$150
(B) Trucks	5 ($250,000)	1 ($50,000)	Rented Truck ($200)	$200
(C)Acres of Land	5 ($5,000)	1 ($1,000)	Rented Premises $500	$500
(D) Staff	30 ($30,000)	5 ($5,000)	2 ($2,000)	$2,000
(E) Cash Capital	$5,000	$3,500	$200	$200
Total	$300,000	$60,000	$3,000	$3,000

In the table above, we entered the goals of our vision to own a brick factory worth three hundred thousand dollars. The ojectives are entered into the first column. The total quantity and value of the factors of production that we desire to acquire is entered into the second column. In the third column, we estimate the minimum quantity required starting our brick factory. Assuming we cannot afford the minimum quantity, we must seek out the substitute to these and enter them in the fourth column. In the fifth column, we enter what assets we can afford in respect of every objective. The vision of building a brick factory worth three hundred thousand dollars might have seemed impossible considering the enormous amount of capital required. The vertical table of objectives, however, has succeeded in breaking down this vision so that we can now begin our brick factory with only sixty thousand dollars. This is twenty percent of our vision. Better still, we can use the substitute column, which further reduces the cost of starting up our brick industry to only three thousand dollars! Here we only need one percent of the actual value of our ultimate vision to start off. The impossible vision is made possible by the table.

Achieving Objectives

"And the LORD answered me, and said, write the vision, and make it plain upon tables, that he may run that reads it. For the vision is yet for an appointed time, but at the end it shall speak, and not lie: though it tarry, wait for it; because it will surely come, it will not tarry" Habakkuk 2:2-3.

This revelation of the prophet Habakkuk teaches that there is a relationship between purpose and time. You must pursue your vision within the context of time. Assuming you can begin this brick factory with the one percent capital required, you must set periodic targets for yourself. For instance, you could set a target to achieve one percent increase in your capital base every quarter.

Whenever the capital base of the factory increases by one percent, it is an indication of progress. Every quarter brings us closer to the achievement of our ultimate factory worth three hundred thousand dollars. Assuming the capital base does not appreciate by the one percent target in a particular quarter, it becomes cause for an investigation. We will have to find out whether it was a physical management flaw or a spiritual cause. Physical flaws could include improper recording of transactions, low productivity, negligence etc. Spiritual flaws could include delay and non-payment of tithes, a dwindling prayer life, failure to observe covenant requirements, spiritual attacks etc.

We must certainly monitor and evaluate our endeavors periodically to foster the achievement of our purposes within the timeframe of our objectives. Divine purposes must be fulfilled during our lifetime here on earth. Our periodic targets increase our drive to work hard towards achieving the vision. Constant monitoring and evaluation help to avert losses in our ventures.

The moment you take the bold initiative to pursue purpose, there is the tendency to invest every financial resource which comes your way into the fulfillment of this purpose. This new business becomes your burden, hence the desire to make every effort to ensure success within the shortest possible time. Naturally, you cut down on your domestic expenditure in favor of your business investments. However, when you delay your pursuit of purpose because you are anticipating that a great financial miracle must come your way to enable you to set up your vision, you frustrate God's plan for your life. Let us look at some reasons why God wants you to start pursuing divine purpose as soon as possible:

Sanctification: God wants you to develop skill in the execution of this mission, which usually takes some time to achieve. He wants you to learn how to effectively mobilize and deploy resources for an investment. Also, the diligence of working with only that which meets the criteria of divine principles executed in the spirit of excellence.

Consecration: This is the essence of keeping the lifeblood of the organization pure through sacrifice. There are certain opportunities and resources that must be volunteered off by your organization to secure divine favor. Holding on unduly to these opportunities and resources closes doors for the organization.

Anointing: There are conventional and creative ways of administering the resources of an organization. In addition to the conventional methods of financial management, creative prudence is the path the anointing lays out for your specific endeavor to flourish supernaturally.

Royalty: The relationship between divine time and purpose is a necessary competence for any destiny engagement. For your organization to survive and prosper in the face of inevitable economic cycles of booms and slumps, you must develop the discipline to emerge as a competent manager of physical and spiritual resources in the context of divine times and seasons.

Summarily, economic empowerment would become a reality if everyone in the local Church understands the principles of leadership, giving and management. The essential principle here is that everyone in the local Church must aspire to become effective leaders, willing givers, and good stewards.

Lending Principle

"The rich rules over the poor, and the borrower is servant to the lender." Proverbs 22:7

Have you noticed that whenever you go out to shop at the mall, they are more interested in selling you a shop credit card than the wares for which are in business? Most of the big retail shops have established banks or lending divisions because of the great benefits of being a lender. First, these companies know that if they extend credit to you, your future patronage of their store is guaranteed. Second, they secure their future by lending to you, knowing that assuming they do not sell goods again, you will be working hard to pay them the credit they extended to you. The interest rate you pay on the credit extended to you is enough income streams for the owners of the retail corporation even if they do not sell goods again. In effect, the corporate world has engaged the lending principle to their full advantage. For this reason, I encourage Christians as much as possible to use credit cards primarily for investment expenditure. Learn to save money for domestic expenses like clothes, furniture, entertainment systems, holiday trips, food and so on.

Just like the secular corporations who have found the wisdom behind lending to potential customers as strategy to engage their loyal patronage and secure their financial future, every Christian must develop the mindset of lending. If a fellow believer requests a very huge sum of money as loan, you must apply the wisdom of due diligence. The principle of lending is in no way meant to drag rich believers into a snare of losing their wealth to unscrupulous and scheming believers. In any case, God will bless your endeavor when you lend resources to help fellow believers advance in their pursuits.

"You shall not charge interest to your brother—interest on money or food or anything that is lent out at interest. To a foreigner you may charge interest, but to your brother you shall not charge interest, that the Lord your God may bless you in all to which you set your hand in the land which you are entering to possess." Deuteronomy 23:19-20.

The Israelite was not permitted to charge interest on money or anything that he lent to a fellow Israelite to meet domestic needs. This principle of lending is meant to assist very poor believers to come out of their poverty. Some people only lend to you because they intend to ask a favor from you soon. It is a loan with interest though you do not charge it directly. Give out to the believer because you have your eyes set on God's promise to bless the work of your hands. "Give to him who asks you, and from him who wants to borrow from you do not turn away." Matthew 5:42. Surely, it is because of the blessing that accompanies lending to our fellow believer that the Lord Jesus encourages us to lend. This is an important spiritual truth for the believer who desires to experience supernatural blessings from God. It is unfortunate that many Christians today want quick returns on every kind of help they render to the needy. If they do not receive the reward quickly, they grumble and get bitter. God's blessing enables us to generate more wealth. "He who has a generous eye will be blessed, for he gives of his bread to the poor." Proverbs 22:9. Generosity is the key to obtain supernatural favor for wealth. This kind of wealth does not have any unpleasant consequences attached to it. Many people have asked me, 'I lent money to a fellow believer who is refusing to pay up, what should I do?' Then I ask them this question, 'Were you convicted to give the fellow the money?' If yes, I usually tell them it is saved in their heavenly account and would be released to them in multiplied returns during their season of harvest. If the answer to my question is no, then usually the loan was either given out of pity for the borrower or because of an interest. If it was because of pity, then consider it loaned to the Lord.

"He who has pity on the poor lends to the Lord, And He will pay back what he has given." Proverbs 19:17.

God has a way of paying you what you gave, though it might not necessarily be through the same borrower. He takes responsibility for any debt that comes under the pity category. However, there is a disclaimer notice for loans given out of hidden interests. God is not responsible for the settlement of such outstanding debts.

The Release

"At the end of every seven years you shall grant a release of debts. And this is the form of the release: Every creditor who has lent anything to his neighbor shall release it; he shall not require it of his neighbor or his brother, because it is called the Lord's release. Of a foreigner you may require it; but you shall give up your claim to what is owed by your brother, except when there may be no poor among you; for the Lord will greatly bless you in the land which the Lord your God is giving you to possess as an inheritance— only if you carefully obey the voice of the Lord your God, to observe with care all these commandments which I command you today. For the Lord your God will bless you just as He promised you; you shall lend to many nations, but you shall not borrow; you shall reign over many nations, but they shall not reign over you." Deuteronomy 15:1-6.

The word release is made up of a prefix, 're' and the word 'lease'. 'Re' means to do it again. 'Lease' is the act of giving out something to another to use over a period. We lease buildings, cars, and machines in secular transactions. When a machine is leased to you, you must make use of it as if it were your own, until the time you return the machine to the owner. Our material possessions including clothes, houses, money, cars and so on were secured by divine favor. "For who makes you differ from another? And what do you have that you did not receive? Now if you did indeed receive it, why do you boast as if you had not received it?" 1 Corinthians 4:7. God gave you the things you possess now, for you to become a manager of wealth here on earth. Whenever God leases anything to you, He convicts you after a while to re-lease it on His behalf to another person. The passage spoke about making a release after every seven years. This simply means, 'Under the inspiration of the Holy Spirit every believer who has lent money or anything to another believer shall re-lease it to him'. In secular terms, this is called 'debt cancellation'. As stewards of wealth, the re-lease is the divine mandate for believers to yield when there is an inspiration of the Holy Spirit to cancel debts owed to them by other believers. God instituted this manner of wealth distribution to alleviate poverty in the lives of His children. If you yield yourself to the conviction of the Holy Spirit to re-lease to other believers, you prove yourself a faithful manager of God's blessings.

"He that is faithful in that which is least is faithful in that which is much; and he that is unjust in the least is also unjust in much." Luke 16:10.

God will entrust you with many more material blessings if you are faithful with what you possess now. It is God's desire that you lend and continue lending until you become a habitual lender. "The Lord will open to you His good treasure, the heavens, to give the rain to your land in its season, and to bless all the work of your hand. You shall lend to many nations, but you shall not borrow." Deuteronomy 28:12. God gives the believer the ability to make wealth when he proves himself faithful to divine convictions. It is God's plan that believers must ultimately rise to become lenders and not borrowers. Every believer must graduate from borrowing and climb up to God's place of prominence in lending. If you cultivate a borrowing habit, you will continue to borrow and end up as a perpetual slave to the lender. Certain nations of this world have applied the principle of canceling debts successfully over the years. These nations are often willing to advance loans and credit facilities to poorer nations. Over a period, the total debt is rescheduled or cancelled under certain conditions. Perhaps, the poor nation must continue to import specific goods from the creditor nation or some other condition that highly favors the creditor nation. Here debt relief is with interest, which is unscriptural. By contrast, the believer must freely release resources because of his faith in God's promise of blessings.

Collateral Security

"You shall not covet your neighbor's house; you shall not covet your neighbor's wife, nor his male servant, nor his female servant, nor his ox, nor his donkey, nor anything that is your neighbor's." Exodus 20:17.

An Israelite was not to desire anything that belonged to his fellow brother with an aim to obtain it. For instance, it was wrong for an Israelite to set his eyes on the nicely located property of another Israelite and agree to lend him money demanding this property as collateral security, all in the hope that this debtor would be unable to pay so he could possess the property.

"No man shall take the nether or the upper millstone to pledge; for he taketh a man's life to pledge." Deuteronomy 24:6.

Furthermore, the believer must not demand impossible collateral as a condition for lending to a fellow believer. The word 'pledge' here is not the same as a vow. Pledge is used here in terms of collateral security for a loan. A nether and upper millstone was how people milled their grain into flour. If a man was not able to pay his debt and his creditors redeemed his millstones, he would not have the means to mill his grain and would starve.

"If you ever take your neighbor's garment as a pledge, you shall return it to him before the sun goes down. For that is his only covering, it is his garment for his skin. What will he sleep in? And it will be that when he cries to Me, I will hear, for I am gracious." Exodus 22:26-27.

Also, if a believer puts up his clothes as security for a loan. Even though you demand it as a way of pressurizing him to settle his debts, you must return it to him by the end of the day. By this principle, God was teaching the Israelites not to demand the necessities of a man's life as security for a loan.

"When you lend your brother anything, you shall not go into his house to get his pledge. You shall stand outside, and the man to whom you lend shall bring the pledge out to you. And if the man is poor, you shall not keep his pledge overnight. You shall in any case return the pledge to him again when the sun goes down, that he may sleep in his own garment and bless you; and it shall be righteousness to you before the Lord your God." Deuteronomy 24:10-13.

Mounting undue pressure on a believer indebted to you is not acceptable to God. It is true that you could be in dire need of the money, but any strong-arm tactics to retrieve the money could cause the indebted believer to cry to God and you may seem as an oppressor. Such a situation will incite the disfavor of God against you. Whatever pressure of need you experience as a lender; God expects you to stand as an intercessor in prayer for your Christian debtors. The power of agreement then sets the stage for divine intervention. "One shall put to flight a thousand, two shall put ten thousand to flight." Deuteronomy 32:30. The negative spiritual forces that work against his ability to fulfill his repayment are overcome through agreement prayer. Also, as a lender you are in the position to objectively review the business practices of the borrower and counsel them to overcome the challenge of indebtedness.

Tithing

"Bring all the tithes into the storehouse, that there may be food in My house, And try Me now in this," Says the Lord of hosts, "If I will not open for you the windows of heaven And pour out for you such blessing That there will not be room enough to receive it. "And I will rebuke the devourer for your sakes, So that he will not destroy the fruit of your ground, Nor shall the vine fail to bear fruit for you in the field," Says the Lord of hosts; "And all nations will call you blessed, For you will be a delightful land," Says the Lord of hosts." Malachi 3:10

While I was being interviewed on a live radio program some time ago, the host asked me to conclude by summing up in one word what I believed was the primary antidote to poverty. Immediately I heard the Holy Spirit whisper in my heart 'tithe'.

"For as the rain comes down, and the snow from heaven, And do not return there, But water the earth, And make it bring forth and bud, That it may give seed to the sower And bread to the eater, So shall My word be that goes forth from My mouth; It shall not return to Me void, But it shall accomplish what I please, And it shall prosper in the thing for which I sent it." Isaiah 55:10,11

The windows of heaven are the source of rain. Rain is significant of God's revelation to man's heart. God opens this window to those who fulfill the covenant of tithing. Tithing believers receive abundance of revelation as blessings. God's revelation enables us to know how to manage our resources to obtain maximum results. Anyone who subscribes to tithing and facilitates God's work on earth would not be denied of divine financial favor.

References

Hebrew – Greek Key Word Study Bible by Spiros Zhodiates
Wilmington's Guide To The Bible by Dr. H.L. Wilmington
Chick-Fil-A – www.chick-fil-a.com
Interstate Batteries – www.interstatebatteries.com
Tyson Foods – www.tysonfoods.com
Forever 21 – www.forever21.com

About The Book And Author

Everyone who earns an income practices some level of enterprise. Households, non-profits, small and big businesses alike must aim to remain solvent. The Church is an ecosystem of all such people who are saved and run some form of enterprise.

While some enterprises survive the downturns of an economic cycle, others fail. Survival could either be due to the nature of industry one belongs to or better still because of proactive measures implemented for resilience in the face of economic downturns. Are there scriptural models by which the Christian can withstand downturns and possibly attain economic growth?

As members of the 'Body of Christ', Christians are connected to one another spiritually and ought also to be interrelated economically. At the inception of the New Testament the apostles leaning on how Jesus tackled situations of lack, established a premise by which they overcame the prevalent financial frustration of their members.

In the last four decades, the author Kenneth Walley has been involved in the academics, practice, and consultancy of business as well as ministry. He developed the cibunet.com platform as a support system for the development and funding of enterprises and projects. He shares in this book, the concepts by which his team at Cibunet Corporation works with Christian Leaders to set up an Economic Empowerment Team in their local Churches as well as Entrepreneurs to grow their enterprises.

Hexagon Quadrilateral